ARTFUL DWELLINGS

Making Your House A Home With Beautiful Art

Neil J Milliner

Books by Neil J Milliner

Dedication

For Jodi DiLiberto— the artist whose vision colors my world.

Your creativity is a reminder that art is not just something we make, but something we live. Your courage, your curiosity, and the way you transform emotion into color continue to inspire every page I write.

To anyone holding this book: If you wish to see the heart behind my own creative life, visit Jodi's work at From the Purple House: www.fromthepurplehouse.art

Her art is a world of its own—vibrant, intuitive, and deeply human. I'm endlessly grateful to walk beside her.

CONTENTS

ARTFUL DWELLINGS

MAKING YOUR HOUSE A HOME WITH BEAUTIFUL ART

COLOR HARMONY: UNVEILING THE BOLD BEAUTY OF INTERIOR DESIGN WITH ARTFUL COLOR BLOCKING

Welcome to a world where hues collide and creativity knows no boundaries! In this blog post, we'll embark on a vibrant journey through the art of color blocking in interior design. From living rooms to bedrooms, discover the transformative power of bold color choices and how art becomes the perfect medium to weave a tapestry of hues. Join us as we explore six sections that will guide you in embracing the bold beauty of color blocking in your home.

Color Blocking 101: Embracing the Basics

In "Color Blocking 101," we delve into the fundamentals of this dynamic design approach. Understand the concept of color blocking and how it involves pairing contrasting or complementary colors to create visually striking combinations. Learn how to choose the right color palette that resonates with your style while making a bold statement in your interior space.

Consider starting small by incorporating color-blocked accessories such as throw pillows, rugs, or wall art to experiment with this exciting design technique. Color Blocking 101 sets the foundation for your journey into a world where each hue plays a crucial role in shaping the overall aesthetic.

Walls Alive: Transformative Color-Blocked Wall Art

In "Walls Alive," we explore the transformative impact of color-blocked wall art on your living spaces. Dive into the world of large canvases adorned with bold geometric shapes and striking color combinations. Discover how art can become the focal point of a room, injecting energy and personality into your home.

Consider choosing art pieces that align with the existing color scheme of your room or opt for contrasting colors to create a captivating visual contrast. Walls Alive showcases the power of color-blocking in turning your walls into dynamic canvases that reflect your design prowess.

Furniture Fusion: Statement Pieces in Every Shade

"Furniture Fusion" takes us on a tour of how color blocking can be incorporated into your furniture choices. From vibrant sofas to eclectic chairs, explore how statement furniture pieces in contrasting or harmonious colors can elevate the overall design of a room. Learn the art of balancing bold choices with the existing decor for a cohesive look.

Consider adding a color-blocked accent chair or investing in a vibrant sofa to instantly transform your living room or bedroom. Furniture Fusion demonstrates how integrating color blocking into your furniture selections can redefine the ambiance of your space.

Room Harmony: Creating Cohesive Spaces with Color

In "Room Harmony," we discuss the importance of creating cohesive spaces through strategic color blocking. Understand how to use color continuity to connect different areas within your home while maintaining a harmonious flow. Learn the secrets of balancing boldness with subtlety to achieve a polished and cohesive interior design.

Consider incorporating a dominant color from one area into the adjoining space through accessories, textiles, or artwork. Room Harmony ensures that your home becomes a seamless blend of bold and harmonious colors, creating an inviting atmosphere for both residents and guests.

Unexpected Pairings: Breaking Conventions with Colorful Surprises

In "Unexpected Pairings," we encourage you to think outside the box and break conventional color rules. Explore the thrill of unexpected color combinations that defy traditional norms. Discover how artful color blocking allows you to infuse your personality into your interior design, making a bold and memorable statement.

Consider pairing unconventional colors like deep teal and mustard yellow or experimenting with unexpected accents that catch the eye. Unexpected Pairings invites you to embrace the element of surprise, allowing your home to reflect your unique sense of style and creativity.

Transcending Seasons: Year-Round Color Brilliance

Our final stop, "Transcending Seasons," explores the timeless beauty of color blocking that transcends seasonal trends. Learn how to create a color palette that remains vibrant and relevant throughout the year. Discover the art of incorporating versatile color schemes that seamlessly adapt to changing seasons without losing their bold appeal.

Consider choosing timeless color combinations like navy and coral or black and white that offer year-round elegance. Transcending Seasons ensures that your color-blocked interior design stands the test of time, providing a vibrant backdrop for your evolving tastes and preferences.

Conclusion:

As we conclude our colorful journey through the world of interior design, remember that color blocking is more than just a design trend—it's a form of self-expression. Whether you're embracing the basics, exploring transformative wall art, fusing colors into furniture, creating room harmony, experimenting with unexpected pairings, or transcending seasons, each section unfolds a layer of the bold beauty that color blocking brings to your living spaces.

BEYOND BOUNDARIES: EMBRACING CUBIST INFLUENCE THROUGH GEOMETRIC SHAPES IN WALL ART

Embark on a visual journey where art transcends traditional boundaries and enters the realm of Cubist influence. In this blog post, "Beyond Boundaries," we delve into the dynamic world of geometric shapes in wall art. From the bold strokes of Picasso to the innovative visions of Braque, discover how Cubist principles can transform your living space into a gallery of avant-garde sophistication. Join us as we explore the playfulness of shapes, the disruption of perspectives, and the harmonious chaos that defines the Cubist movement.

Cubism Unveiled: A Glimpse into Artistic Revolution

Begin our exploration in "Cubism Unveiled," where we take a glimpse into the artistic revolution that gave birth to Cubism. Coined by art critic Louis Vauxcelles in the early 20th century, Cubism shattered traditional notions of representation. Picasso and Braque, pioneers of the movement, embraced the use of geometric shapes to depict multiple viewpoints simultaneously, challenging the linear constraints of reality.

Select wall art pieces that embody the essence of Cubism – fragmented forms, overlapping planes, and a departure from realistic representation. The beauty of Cubism lies in its ability to infuse dynamism and depth into static surfaces, transforming your walls into a canvas of perpetual movement and intrigue.

Geometric Play: Infusing Your Space with Dynamic Shapes

Transition into the second section, "Geometric Play," where we explore the dynamic interplay of shapes in Cubist-inspired wall art. Geometric shapes – triangles, squares, circles – take center stage, forming a language that communicates complexity through simplicity. Consider selecting pieces that experiment with geometric abstraction, using bold lines and vibrant colors to create a sense of rhythm and movement.

Infuse your space with the energy of geometric play, where each shape contributes to the overall composition. Whether through paintings, prints, or sculptures, let the interlocking forms transport you to a realm where boundaries blur, and the language of shapes becomes a celebration of artistic freedom.

Perspective Distorted: Embracing the Chaos of Multiple Views

In the third section, "Perspective Distorted," we dive into the Cubist technique of embracing the chaos of multiple views. Cubism shattered the traditional single-point perspective, allowing artists to depict objects from multiple angles simultaneously. This distortion of perspective created a sense of disarray and complexity, challenging viewers to engage with art on a more cerebral level.

Explore wall art that mirrors the Cubist approach to perspective – fragmented views, disassembled forms, and a celebration of the chaotic beauty within structure. The distortion of perspective invites viewers to engage in a visual dance, deciphering the intricate relationships between shapes and perspectives. Immerse yourself in the world of distorted perspectives and witness how it transforms your living space into an ever-evolving visual puzzle.

Harmonious Chaos: Finding Balance in Cubist Compositions

Move on to "Harmonious Chaos," where we explore the paradoxical concept of finding balance within Cubist compositions. Despite the apparent chaos and fragmentation, Cubist art maintains a sense of order and harmony. This section delves into the delicate balance that artists strike between dissonance and unity, creating compositions that are both visually stimulating and emotionally resonant.

Select wall art pieces that exemplify harmonious chaos – compositions where disparate shapes coexist in a state of equilibrium. The interplay of color, form, and negative space contributes to the overall harmony, turning your walls into a captivating display of structured chaos. Witness how harmonious chaos in Cubist compositions elevates your living space into a realm of avant-garde sophistication.

Beyond the Canvas: Cubist Influence in Home Decor

Enter the fifth section, "Beyond the Canvas," where we explore how Cubist influence extends beyond traditional art mediums and infiltrates home decor. From furniture to textiles, Cubist principles can be seamlessly integrated into various elements of interior design. Consider selecting decor items that echo the geometric language of Cubism, such as patterned rugs, angular furniture, or even wall murals.

Cubist influence in home decor adds a touch of avant-garde sophistication to your living space, creating a cohesive aesthetic that extends beyond the confines of the canvas. Explore the possibilities of infusing Cubist design into your home, turning every corner into a celebration of geometric play and artistic rebellion.

DIY Cubism: Crafting Your Own Geometric Masterpiece

In the final section, "DIY Cubism," we empower you to embark on your own artistic journey by crafting a Cubist-inspired geometric masterpiece. Unleash your creativity by experimenting with shapes, colors, and perspectives. Whether through painting, collage, or mixed-media projects, DIY Cubism allows you to become the artist, breaking free from conventions and expressing your unique vision.

Consider involving family members or friends in DIY projects, turning the creation of a Cubist-inspired masterpiece into a collaborative and enjoyable experience. The joy of DIY Cubism lies not only in the finished creation but also in the process of self-discovery and artistic exploration. Embrace the freedom to craft your own geometric masterpiece, where every stroke and shape becomes a reflection of your artistic rebellion.

Conclusion:

As we conclude our exploration of Cubist influence through geometric shapes in wall art, remember that art has the power to transcend boundaries and challenge conventions. Whether you're drawn to the revolutionary spirit of Cubism, the dynamic play of shapes, the distorted perspectives, harmonious chaos, home decor integration, or the joy of DIY Cubism, each section unveils a facet of the transformative power that Cubist principles hold in elevating your living space into a realm of avant-garde sophistication.

ABSTRACT WONDERS: A FRIENDLY GUIDE TO INTERPRETING AND APPRECIATING ABSTRACT ART

Navigating the vibrant world of abstract art is like embarking on a visual adventure, where colors, shapes, and forms dance in harmony. This friendly guide is your compass, offering tips and insights on interpreting and appreciating abstract art, transforming what may seem elusive into a canvas of wonder.

1: Decoding the Abstract Language: Understanding Forms and Shapes

Abstract art often speaks a language of its own, with forms and shapes taking center stage. This section provides a friendly introduction to decoding this abstract language. From geometric shapes to fluid forms, understanding the visual elements is the first step in appreciating abstract artworks. Friendly insights on the use of color, line, and texture contribute to a nuanced understanding of how artists communicate emotions and ideas through abstract compositions. As you delve into the world of forms and shapes, allow your instincts to guide you, and embrace the beauty of interpretation.

Transitioning seamlessly between the canvas and the observer, this section encourages art enthusiasts to view abstract forms as a visual vocabulary, inviting personal connections and interpretations.

2: Color Symphony: Embracing the Emotional Palette

Colors in abstract art are more than just pigments; they are a symphony of emotions. This section explores the emotional palette of abstract artworks, guiding you to interpret the feelings evoked by different colors. Friendly tips on understanding color contrasts, harmonies, and the psychological impact of hues empower you to engage with abstract art on a visceral level. As you immerse yourself in the color symphony, allow the emotions stirred by each shade to guide your interpretation, recognizing that abstract artists often use color as a powerful tool for expression.

Much like a musical composition, abstract art invites you to embrace the emotional notes woven into the canvas, creating a rich and resonant experience that goes beyond the visual.

3: Texture Tales: Exploring the Tactile Dimension

The tactile dimension of abstract art adds a layer of intrigue and depth to the viewing experience. This section invites you to explore the texture tales within abstract artworks. From smooth surfaces to textured layers, understanding how artists play with tactile elements enhances your appreciation of their creative choices. Friendly insights on the use of impasto, collage, and mixed media contribute to a deeper understanding of the tactile dimension. As you run your eyes over the textured surface, consider the artist's intention behind each stroke and the added storytelling dimension that textures bring to abstract art.

Transitioning between the visual and tactile, this section encourages art enthusiasts to engage with abstract art through more than just sight, allowing the sense of touch to amplify the interpretative experience.

4: The Dance of Lines: Finding Movement and Direction

Lines in abstract art are not just boundaries; they are pathways that guide the viewer's gaze. This section delves into the dance of lines, offering friendly insights on interpreting movement, direction, and rhythm within abstract compositions. Understanding how artists use lines to create flow and energy adds a dynamic layer to your appreciation of abstract artworks. Friendly tips on recognizing different types of lines and their symbolic meanings empower you to decipher the intentional pathways that artists construct. As you follow the dance of lines, let your eyes trace the artist's choreography, finding both structure and spontaneity within the intricate movements.

Much like a dance performance, abstract art invites you to be an active participant, moving along the lines and engaging with the visual choreography in a way that transcends traditional boundaries.

5: Conceptual Narratives: Unveiling Abstract Stories

Abstract art often conceals narratives that unfold upon closer inspection. This section guides you through unveiling conceptual narratives within abstract compositions. Friendly insights on understanding the artist's intent, recognizing symbolism, and interpreting abstract stories contribute to a narrative-driven appreciation of these artworks. As you engage with abstract pieces, consider the possibility that each stroke and shape may be part of a larger story waiting to be discovered. Embrace the ambiguity and allow your imagination to connect the dots, creating a personal narrative that adds layers of meaning to the abstract canvas.

Transitioning between the enigmatic and the revealed, this section encourages art enthusiasts to view abstract art as a visual puzzle, inviting them to uncover the hidden stories and concepts embedded within the composition.

6: Personal Reflections: The Beauty of Subjectivity in Abstract Art

The beauty of abstract art lies in its subjectivity, inviting personal reflections and interpretations. This section celebrates the individuality of perception and encourages you to trust your instincts when engaging with abstract artworks. Friendly insights on embracing ambiguity, allowing for multiple interpretations, and appreciating the diversity of responses within the art community contribute to a liberating view of abstract art. As you reflect on your personal responses, recognize that there is no right or wrong way to interpret abstract art; each perspective adds a unique brushstroke to the collective appreciation of these captivating creations.

Much like a mirror reflecting the viewer's thoughts, abstract art invites you to appreciate the beauty of subjectivity, where every interpretation becomes a valid and valuable contribution to the dialogue.

THE ART OF SEASONS: TRANSFORMING YOUR HOME'S VIBE AND VALUE

Embracing the Ever-Changing Canvas of Seasonal Wall Art

Welcome to a journey through the seasons, where the art on your walls becomes a dynamic expression of nature's ever-changing beauty. In "The Art of Seasons," we explore how incorporating seasonal wall art can not only alter the atmosphere of your home but also add significant value. Let's dive into the magic of seasonal transformations that go beyond aesthetics, creating a living, breathing canvas within your living space.

"Springtime Awakening: Floral Frescoes and Pastel Hues"

In "Springtime Awakening," discover the enchantment of bringing the vibrancy of spring indoors. Explore how floral-themed wall art and pastel color palettes can infuse your home with a sense of renewal and vitality. Uncover the psychological impact of spring-inspired artwork on mood and well-being, creating an atmosphere of freshness that resonates with both inhabitants and potential buyers.

"Summer Radiance: Coastal Vibes and Sun-Kissed Tones"

"Summer Radiance" invites you to bask in the warmth of coastal vibes and sun-kissed tones. Explore the use of beach-themed art and a palette inspired by the sun-drenched hues of summer. Dive into the ways in which seasonal wall art can evoke the carefree spirit of summer, turning your home into a retreat that appeals to a wide range of tastes.

"Autumnal Elegance: Nature's Palette and Cozy Textures"

In "Autumnal Elegance," witness the transformation of your space with nature's palette and cozy textures. Delve into the rich, warm tones and earthy artwork that define autumn. Learn how these seasonal elements not only create a cozy and inviting ambiance but also contribute to the perceived comfort and value of your home.

"Winter Whimsy: Snowy Landscapes and Cool Tones"

"Winter Whimsy" brings the serene beauty of snowy landscapes and cool tones into focus. Explore how winter-themed art can evoke a sense of tranquility and simplicity. Understand the visual impact of cool color palettes on creating a calm and sophisticated atmosphere, turning your home into a winter wonderland that captivates potential buyers.

"Investing in Seasonal Flexibility: Versatility for All-Year Appeal"

"Investing in Seasonal Flexibility" explores the concept of creating a home that seamlessly adapts to the seasons. Discover the value of versatile seasonal wall art that allows you to effortlessly transition from one season to the next. Understand how this flexibility appeals to a broader audience, making your home a year-round haven for potential buyers.

"Beyond Aesthetics: The Tangible Impact on Property Value"

In "Beyond Aesthetics," we unravel the tangible impact of seasonal wall art on property value. Explore how the adaptability of your home to the seasons translates into enhanced market appeal. Understand the psychology of buyers and how the changing artwork aligns with their evolving preferences, making your property stand out in the real estate market.

FLOATING SHELVES AND ART: COMBINING STORAGE AND DISPLAY

Welcome to a world where functionality meets aesthetics. In "Floating Shelves and Art: Combining Storage and Display," we delve into the creative synergy between storage solutions and artistic expressions. Discover how floating shelves not only declutter your space but also provide a canvas for showcasing your favorite artworks.

The Art of Organization: Floating Shelves as Stylish Storage

In "The Art of Organization," we explore how floating shelves offer a sleek and stylish solution for organizing your space. Say goodbye to traditional storage units and embrace the modern appeal of floating shelves. Discover how these minimalist wonders can transform your walls into functional yet fashionable storage spaces.

Consider incorporating floating shelves into your home office, living room, or bedroom to keep your essentials within reach while maintaining a visually appealing environment. The Art of Organization demonstrates that storage can be an art form in itself.

Designing with Depth: Creating Visual Interest on Your Walls

In "Designing with Depth," we delve into the visual impact of combining floating shelves with art. Explore how the varying depths of shelves can create dynamic displays, adding depth and interest to your walls. Learn the art of arranging artworks, books, and decorative items to achieve a harmonious and visually engaging composition.

Consider experimenting with asymmetrical arrangements to bring a sense of spontaneity to your display. Designing with Depth introduces you to the world of three-dimensional wall art that goes beyond the conventional.

Gallery Wall Redux: Curating Collections on Floating Shelves

In "Gallery Wall Redux," we reimagine the classic gallery wall concept using floating shelves. Uncover the flexibility that shelves offer in curating and rearranging your art collection. From rotating seasonal displays to showcasing themed collections, discover how floating shelves provide an ever-evolving gallery experience.

Consider mixing framed artwork with small sculptures, plants, and personal mementos to create a curated and personalized gallery wall. Gallery Wall Redux inspires you to turn your walls into a constantly evolving art gallery.

Functional Fusions: Combining Shelves with Functional Art

In "Functional Fusions," we explore the integration of functional art with floating shelves. Discover how shelves can become a canvas for art that serves a purpose, such as unique bookends, plant holders, or even concealed storage solutions. Dive into the world of creative collaborations between form and function.

Consider incorporating floating shelves that double as planters or incorporating magnetic surfaces for displaying magnetic artwork. Functional Fusions demonstrates that art doesn't have to be purely decorative; it can also enhance the functionality of your living space.

Styling Secrets: Tips for Arranging Art on Floating Shelves

In "Styling Secrets," we unravel the tips and tricks for arranging art on floating shelves like a design pro. From achieving balance to playing with scale, discover the secrets to creating visually appealing displays that captivate the eye. Learn how to mix textures, colors, and shapes for a harmonious and curated look.

Consider rotating your art pieces periodically to keep the display fresh and engaging. Styling Secrets empowers you to become your own curator and transform your space into a design masterpiece.

DIY Delights: Crafting Your Own Floating Shelves and Art

In "DIY Delights," we embark on a creative journey, exploring how you can craft your own floating shelves and personalized art pieces. Dive into simple DIY projects that allow you to customize your storage and display solutions, adding a personal touch to your home.

Consider repurposing old wooden planks or exploring unconventional materials for your DIY floating shelves. DIY Delights inspires you to unleash your creativity and create functional art that reflects your unique style.

Conclusion:

As we conclude our exploration of "Floating Shelves and Art: Combining Storage and Display," let your home become a canvas for both organization and artistic expression. From The Art of Organization to DIY Delights, each section showcases the endless possibilities when functionality and aesthetics unite. Embrace the synergy of floating shelves and art, transforming your living space into a dynamic and visually captivating haven.

BEYOND THE THRESHOLD: ELEVATING CURB APPEAL WITH OUTDOOR WALL ART

The Artful Greeting

Welcome to "Beyond the Threshold," where we embark on a journey to explore the transformative power of outdoor wall art in enhancing your home's curb appeal. In this guide, we'll uncover creative ideas, innovative designs, and expert tips to turn the exterior of your house into a captivating canvas that welcomes and wows. Get ready to discover how a touch of artistry can elevate your home's first impression, making a statement that lingers long after guests have crossed the threshold.

1: "The Power of First Impressions"

In "The Power of First Impressions," we unravel the psychology behind curb appeal and how outdoor wall art plays a pivotal role. Explore the impact of a visually striking exterior in creating a positive and lasting first impression on guests and potential buyers alike. Discover how the careful selection and placement of outdoor art can set the tone for the entire aesthetic experience of your home, making it an inviting haven from the moment one approaches.

Transforming your home's exterior isn't just about aesthetics; it's about crafting an experience that resonates with those who encounter it. Dive into the artful world of first impressions and learn how to use outdoor wall art strategically to captivate, charm, and leave an indelible mark.

2: "Natural Elements as Artistic Allies"

Embark on "Natural Elements as Artistic Allies," where we explore the fusion of nature and art to enhance your curb appeal. Delve into creative ideas that seamlessly integrate outdoor wall art with the surrounding environment, using natural elements as both inspiration and backdrop. Discover how incorporating materials like wood, stone, or even living greenery into your outdoor art installations can create a harmonious and visually appealing atmosphere.

The marriage of natural elements and art isn't just about aesthetics; it's about cultivating an organic and balanced exterior. Uncover how to leverage the beauty of the outdoors to amplify your curb appeal, creating a welcoming environment that seamlessly integrates with the surrounding landscape.

3: "Artistic Architectural Accents"

In "Artistic Architectural Accents," we explore how outdoor wall art can serve as architectural enhancements, transforming the façade of your home into a masterpiece. Discover unique ideas for incorporating art into the structure itself, whether through custom-designed elements, intricate murals, or creative installations that celebrate the architectural features of your home. Learn how these artistic accents can elevate the overall design, making your house a standout in the neighborhood.

Architectural accents aren't just about embellishments; they're about turning your home into a work of art. Explore the possibilities of merging art and architecture to create a distinctive curb appeal that showcases the unique personality and style of your property.

4: "Seasonal Statements: The Ever-Changing Canvas"

Journey into "Seasonal Statements," where we explore the dynamic nature of outdoor wall art that evolves with the seasons. Discover how to use seasonal themes and adaptable installations to keep your curb appeal fresh and captivating throughout the year. From vibrant springtime florals to cozy winter vignettes, learn how to curate a rotating gallery that mirrors the changing seasons and captures the attention of passersby.

Seasonal statements aren't just about décor changes; they're about celebrating the beauty of every season. Explore how embracing the ephemerality of outdoor art can create a sense of anticipation and excitement, making your home a focal point in any weather.

5: "DIY Delights: Personalizing Your Outdoor Art"

In "DIY Delights," we unleash the artist in you, exploring the joy of creating personalized outdoor art installations. Discover how do-it-yourself projects can add a touch of uniqueness and charm to your curb appeal, turning your outdoor walls into a canvas for your creativity. From hand-painted murals to repurposed materials, learn how to infuse your personality into every stroke and detail, creating a home that truly reflects who you are.

DIY delights aren't just about saving money; they're about infusing your home with a personal touch. Dive into the world of self-expression and learn how to transform your outdoor space into a reflection of your passions, memories, and individuality.

6: "Lighting the Night: Illuminating Outdoor Art"

Conclude our journey with "Lighting the Night," where we explore the impact of outdoor lighting on your artful exterior. Discover how well-placed lights can enhance the visibility and allure of your outdoor wall art during the evening hours, creating a captivating scene that extends the impact of your curb appeal into the night. From subtle uplighting to dramatic spotlights, learn how to play with light to create a mesmerizing ambiance around your home.

Lighting the night isn't just about visibility; it's about extending the magic of your curb appeal into the evening hours. Uncover the secrets of outdoor lighting and learn how to make your home a beacon of artistic allure that captivates both day and night.

GALLERY GLEAM: UNVEILING THE SECRETS TO CREATING A STUNNING GALLERY WALL

Step into a world where your walls become an ever-evolving masterpiece, a gallery that tells the story of your life and passions. In this blog post, we'll dive into the art of creating a stunning gallery wall – a curated display that transcends mere decoration and becomes a symphony of visual delight. From inspiration to execution, join us on a journey to unlock the secrets that turn your walls into an artistic panorama, weaving together memories, creativity, and your unique style.

1. Gallery Wall Unveiled: The Magic of Creating a Stunning Display:

The magic of creating a stunning gallery wall lies in the seamless integration of diverse elements into a harmonious display. Begin by envisioning the narrative you want your wall to tell. Whether it's a collection of family photos, an assortment of art pieces, or a thematic display, the key is to infuse personality into the arrangement. The gallery wall is your canvas; let it be a reflection of your life, experiences, and aesthetic sensibilities.

Consider the layout and dimensions of the wall. A gallery wall doesn't necessarily need to cover the entire expanse; it can be a focal point or an accentuating feature. Experiment with different arrangements before settling on the final display. The goal is to create a visual flow that captivates the eye, inviting onlookers to explore the individual stories within the collective display.

2. The Art of Assembling: Gallery Wall Inspiration and Tips:

Assembling a gallery wall is an art form that blends inspiration with meticulous planning. Start by gathering inspiration from various sources – Pinterest boards, interior design magazines, or even art galleries. Explore different styles, arrangements, and themes that resonate with you. Gallery wall inspiration can come from anywhere, so allow your creativity to roam freely.

Consider the variety of elements you want to include in your gallery wall. Mix and match framed photographs, art prints, paintings, and even three-dimensional objects for added texture. Think about the color palette; harmonize or contrast, depending on the desired effect. The art of assembling a gallery wall involves finding a balance between unity and diversity, creating a visually arresting display that celebrates the unique stories behind each piece.

3. Ideas for a Beautiful Gallery Wall Display:

Ideas for a beautiful gallery wall display are as diverse as the individuals curating them. One popular approach is the symmetrical arrangement, where frames and artworks are meticulously aligned to create a structured and polished look. This works particularly well with a collection of similar-sized pieces or a series of photographs.

For a more eclectic vibe, consider the salon-style gallery wall. This involves an artful mix of differently sized frames and varied arrangements. The result is a visually dynamic display that feels curated yet spontaneous. Experiment with overlapping frames, different shapes, and even interspersing decorative objects like mirrors or clocks.

4. Personal Touch: Infusing Your Gallery Wall with Individuality:

The true allure of a gallery wall lies in its ability to reflect your individuality and personal touch. Infuse your gallery wall with pieces that hold sentimental value – family photographs, mementos from travels, or artworks created by loved ones. These personal touches add depth and authenticity to the display, turning it into a living narrative of your life.

Consider incorporating elements that speak to your passions and hobbies. If you're a nature enthusiast, intersperse botanical prints or landscapes within the arrangement. For book lovers, framed book covers or literary quotes can become intriguing additions. The key is to make the gallery wall an extension of your personality, allowing it to evolve and grow with your experiences and interests.

5. Curating a Timeless Display: Tips for Long-lasting Gallery Wall Appeal:

Creating a gallery wall is not just about the here and now; it's about curating a timeless display that retains its appeal over the years. Choose frames and mats that are classic and versatile, allowing for flexibility in updating and rearranging the display. Consider a neutral color palette for the frames to ensure they complement various artworks and photographs.

To maintain a cohesive look, stick to a common thread that ties the pieces together – whether it's a consistent color scheme, a specific theme, or a recurring element. This ensures that as you add or change pieces, the gallery wall retains its visual harmony. Regularly assess the arrangement and update it to reflect your evolving tastes, ensuring that the display remains a dynamic reflection of your style.

6. The Finishing Touch: Enhancing Your Gallery Wall with Thoughtful Details:

The finishing touch is where the magic happens – it's about enhancing your gallery wall with thoughtful details that elevate the overall aesthetic. Pay attention to the spacing between frames, ensuring a balanced and visually appealing arrangement. Experiment with different hanging styles – consider aligning frames along an imaginary line for a clean look or creating a more organic flow with irregular spacing.

Add depth to your gallery wall by incorporating elements like shadow boxes or floating shelves. These provide opportunities to showcase three-dimensional objects, adding a tactile and dynamic dimension to the display. Don't forget about lighting – consider installing picture lights or using strategically placed lamps to highlight specific pieces and create a captivating play of shadows.

Conclusion:

As we conclude our journey into the world of gallery wall creation, remember that the true beauty lies in the process – from inspiration to execution, from assembling diverse elements to infusing your personal touch. A stunning gallery wall is not just a decorative feature; it's a living tapestry that evolves with your life, telling stories, sparking memories, and celebrating your unique style. So, embark on this artistic adventure and transform your walls into a gallery of endless possibilities.

COLOR CANVAS: NAVIGATING THE EMOTIONAL LANDSCAPE OF WALL ART

Welcome to the kaleidoscopic world of color psychology in wall art, where the hues you choose become the brushstrokes that paint the emotional canvas of your living space. In this blog post, we'll delve into the fascinating realm of the emotional impact of colors in art, exploring the ways in which your wall decor can evoke feelings, set moods, and create a harmonious atmosphere. From the warm embrace of reds to the calming presence of blues, join us on a journey of understanding the psychological effects of colors and how you can use them to transform your home into a haven of emotions.

1. The Palette of Emotions: Unraveling Color Psychology in Wall Art:

The palette of emotions begins with an exploration of color psychology in wall art. Each color carries its own set of emotional connotations, triggering specific feelings and responses. For instance, warm colors like reds, oranges, and yellows are associated with energy, passion, and vibrancy, making them ideal for spaces where you want to create a sense of warmth and dynamism. On the other hand, cool colors such as blues and greens evoke calmness, serenity, and introspection, making them perfect for spaces where relaxation and tranquility are desired.

Understanding the psychological impact of colors allows you to curate a wall art display that aligns with the emotional ambiance you wish to create in each room. Whether it's the invigorating burst of a sunrise-inspired artwork in the living room or the soothing blues of a seascape in the bedroom, the palette of emotions becomes your guide in transforming your home into a space that resonates with your desired feelings.

2. The Vibrant Language of Reds: Harnessing Energy and Passion in Wall Decor:

Reds, the vibrant and bold hue that symbolizes passion and energy, have a profound impact on the emotional landscape of wall art. Incorporating reds into your wall decor can inject a sense of dynamism and vitality into the space. A large red canvas in the dining area can stimulate conversation and appetite, while red accents in the bedroom add a touch of intensity and passion.

The key to harnessing the emotional impact of reds lies in balance. Too much red can be overwhelming, while the right amount creates a stimulating and invigorating atmosphere. Consider pairing reds with neutral tones or complementary colors to create a harmonious and visually appealing display. The language of reds in wall art is a powerful tool for infusing energy and passion into your home, creating spaces that exude warmth and intensity.

3. Tranquil Blues: Creating Serenity and Calmness with Cool Tones:

Enter the tranquil world of blues, where cool tones create a sense of serenity and calmness in wall art. Blues are known for their ability to evoke feelings of peace, relaxation, and introspection. Incorporating shades of blue into your wall decor can transform your living space into a soothing oasis, perfect for areas where you want to unwind and destress.

Consider a large blue abstract painting in the bedroom to create a serene and tranquil ambiance. Blues also work well in spaces dedicated to quiet reflection, such as a reading nook or meditation corner. Mixing different shades of blue adds depth and complexity to your wall art display, allowing you to play with the emotional nuances of this cool and calming color.

4. The Uplifting Power of Yellows: Infusing Joy and Optimism into Wall Art:

Yellows, the color of sunshine and warmth, have the power to infuse joy and optimism into your wall art. This cheerful hue is associated with positivity, energy, and a sense of happiness. Incorporating yellows into your living space can create an uplifting atmosphere, making it an ideal choice for areas where you want to foster a sense of optimism and vibrancy.

Consider a gallery wall of yellow-themed artworks in a workspace to boost creativity and motivation. In the kitchen, yellows can add a touch of energy, making the space feel inviting and lively. The key to utilizing the emotional impact of yellows is to strike a balance – too much can be overpowering, while the right amount brings a delightful burst of sunshine into your home.

5. Nature's Greens: Fostering Balance and Harmony in Wall Decor:

Green, the color of nature and balance, fosters a harmonious atmosphere in wall decor. This versatile hue is associated with growth, renewal, and tranquility. Incorporating greens into your living space can create a sense of balance and connection with the natural world. From deep forest greens to refreshing mint tones, the spectrum of greens offers a range of emotional nuances.

Consider a botanical-themed gallery wall in the living room to bring the outdoors in, creating a space that feels fresh and revitalizing. Greens work well in spaces dedicated to relaxation, such as bedrooms or reading corners. Whether through botanical prints, landscape paintings, or abstract green hues, nature's greens become a powerful tool for fostering balance and harmony in your home.

6. Neutral Elegance: Using Whites, Grays, and Browns for Timeless Sophistication:

Amidst the vibrant spectrum, neutral tones of whites, grays, and browns offer timeless sophistication in wall decor. These hues create a backdrop of elegance, allowing other colors to shine or providing a serene canvas on their own. Whites evoke a sense of purity and simplicity, grays offer a modern and sophisticated vibe, while browns provide warmth and grounding.

Incorporating neutral tones into your wall art allows for versatility and adaptability. A gallery wall with black and white photography exudes classic elegance, while abstract artworks in shades of gray add a contemporary touch. The key to using neutral tones lies in the interplay of textures and shades, creating a visually rich and sophisticated display that stands the test of time.

Conclusion:

As we conclude our exploration of the psychology of colors in wall art, remember that the emotional impact of colors goes beyond aesthetics – it transforms your home into a living canvas of emotions, moods, and personality. Whether you're infusing passion with reds, creating serenity with blues, or fostering optimism with yellows, the colors you choose become the emotional heartbeat of your living space. So, embark on this colorful journey, and let your walls tell the story of your emotions.

ARTISTRY IN SMALL SPACES: MAXIMIZING IMPACT WITH WALL DECOR

Welcome to the enchanting world of transforming small spaces into curated havens of style and personality. In this blog post, we'll explore the artistry of using wall art to maximize impact, turning petite rooms into visual masterpieces that captivate and inspire. From strategic placement to the choice of art styles, join us on a journey of creativity, uncovering the secrets to transforming small spaces through the transformative power of wall decor.

1. Petite Elegance: Making a Big Statement with Small Spaces:

Petite spaces may be limited in square footage, but they offer a canvas of opportunity for making a big statement through artistry. Begin by considering the purpose of the space – is it a cozy reading nook, a compact home office, or a snug entryway? Small spaces benefit from a carefully curated selection of wall art that enhances the ambiance without overwhelming the proportions.

Choosing art with vertical or horizontal lines can visually elongate or widen the space, depending on the layout. Opt for lighter colors to create an airy and open feel, while strategically placed mirrors can add depth and reflect natural light. The key is to embrace petite elegance by selecting wall decor that complements the room's function and enhances its aesthetic appeal.

2. Artful Illusions: Using Wall Art to Create Depth and Dimension:

The magic of transforming small spaces lies in the artful use of illusions, and wall art becomes a powerful tool in creating depth and dimension. Consider incorporating artworks with perspective, such as cityscape prints or abstract pieces that draw the eye into the distance. Murals or large-scale art installations that create a focal point can also give the illusion of more space.

Mirrors are a particularly effective trick in the artful playbook for small spaces. Placed strategically, mirrors can reflect light, making the room feel brighter and more spacious. Additionally, mirrored wall art adds a touch of glamour and sophistication. By mastering the art of illusions through wall decor, you elevate small spaces beyond their physical constraints, creating an environment that feels expansive and visually engaging.

3. The Bold and the Beautiful: Making a Statement with Statement Pieces:

In the realm of small spaces, the mantra is often "less is more," but that doesn't mean sacrificing impact. The bold and the beautiful come together when you strategically incorporate statement pieces into your wall decor. Choose one or two impactful artworks that become the focal point of the room – a vibrant abstract painting, an oversized photograph, or a unique sculpture.

Statement pieces add personality and character to small spaces, transforming them from merely functional to aesthetically captivating. Consider selecting art that resonates with your style and evokes emotions. The bold and the beautiful in wall decor become conversation starters, drawing attention away from the limited square footage and towards the visual feast of creativity.

4. Vertical Mastery: Using Height to Expand Horizons in Small Spaces:

Unlock the secret of vertical mastery to expand horizons in small spaces. When working with limited floor space, the vertical dimension becomes your ally. Choose wall art that emphasizes height – vertical paintings, tall bookshelves with integrated art, or a gallery wall that draws the eye upward. This vertical emphasis not only creates the illusion of height but also draws attention away from the constrained footprint.

Consider floor-to-ceiling bookshelves adorned with a mix of books and art pieces to maximize vertical impact. Install long, narrow artworks that guide the gaze upward, emphasizing the vertical lines in the room. Vertical mastery in small spaces is about creating a sense of grandeur and elegance through thoughtful placement and strategic selection of wall art that emphasizes height.

5. Multipurpose Magic: Using Functional Wall Decor in Small Spaces:

Small spaces thrive on multipurpose magic, and functional wall decor becomes the key to this transformative alchemy. Opt for pieces that serve both an aesthetic and practical purpose – floating shelves with integrated art, a wall-mounted desk with a gallery of inspiration above, or decorative hooks that double as a display for hats or accessories.

Functional wall decor not only maximizes impact but also contributes to the overall efficiency and organization of small spaces. Consider wall-mounted organizers, magnetic boards for notes and reminders, or a combination of framed prints and corkboards for a personalized touch. Multipurpose magic allows small spaces to fulfill a variety of needs while remaining visually appealing and well-curated.

6. Cohesive Harmony: Creating a Unified Look with Coordinated Wall Art:

The final touch in the artistry of transforming small spaces is achieving cohesive harmony through coordinated wall art. Select a unifying theme, color palette, or style that ties together the various pieces in the room. This could be a series of artworks with a similar motif, a monochromatic color scheme, or a collection of framed photographs that share a common theme.

Cohesive harmony ensures that the wall decor in small spaces works together seamlessly, creating a unified look that feels intentional and curated. Avoid overcrowding the walls; instead, opt for a balanced arrangement that contributes to the overall flow of the room. The artful coordination of wall decor becomes the finishing stroke, turning small spaces into harmonious retreats of style and sophistication.

Conclusion:

As we conclude our journey into the artistry of using wall art to maximize impact in small spaces, remember that creativity knows no boundaries. Whether through illusions, statement pieces, vertical mastery, functional decor, or cohesive harmony, wall art becomes the transformative brush that turns petite rooms into visual masterpieces. Embrace the challenge, think outside the box, and let your walls tell the story of ingenuity and style in every square inch.

ECLECTIC ELEGANCE: MASTERING THE ART OF MIXING AND MATCHING WALL GALLERIES

Step into the vibrant world of eclectic elegance, where the art of mixing and matching transforms your walls into a gallery of diverse stories and styles. In this blog post, we'll embark on a journey of creativity, exploring the magic of combining different artworks, frames, and styles to create a visually captivating and uniquely personal wall gallery. From understanding the fundamentals to breaking the rules, join us in mastering the art of eclectic wall galleries that speak to your individuality and make a bold statement in your home.

1. The Symphony of Styles: Embracing Diversity in Wall Galleries:

The symphony of styles is the heartbeat of eclectic wall galleries. Embrace diversity by bringing together a variety of artistic expressions, from contemporary prints to vintage photographs, abstract paintings to framed quotes. The key is to celebrate the unique character of each piece while ensuring they harmonize as part of a cohesive whole. Don't be afraid to mix genres and eras – the beauty lies in the unexpected juxtapositions that add layers of intrigue to your gallery.

Consider incorporating different mediums, such as framed textiles, mirrors, or even three-dimensional objects like plates or small sculptures. The symphony of styles is about creating a dynamic conversation between the various elements, turning your wall gallery into a rich tapestry of visual interest. Each piece contributes a distinct note, and together, they compose a melody that reflects your eclectic taste.

2. Beyond Frames: Exploring Creative Display Options for Wall Galleries:

The world of eclectic wall galleries extends beyond traditional frames, inviting you to explore creative display options that add flair and personality to your collection. Consider floating shelves as a versatile platform for arranging a mix of framed artworks, small sculptures, and decorative objects. This unconventional approach adds depth and dimension to your gallery while allowing for easy rearrangement.

Another creative option is the use of clipboards or wire grids for an effortlessly chic and modern display. Clipboards provide a flexible and interchangeable way to showcase prints, photographs, and even small sketches. Wire grids offer an industrial and minimalist aesthetic, allowing you to clip or hang various pieces in a grid pattern. Beyond frames, these creative display options become an integral part of the eclectic narrative, elevating your wall gallery to a new level of artistic expression.

3. Finding Common Threads: Creating Unity in Eclectic Wall Galleries:

Amidst the diversity of styles and display options, finding common threads is the secret to creating unity in eclectic wall galleries. Identify a unifying element that ties the various pieces together – whether it's a consistent color palette, a recurring theme, or a shared aesthetic. This common thread provides a visual anchor that allows the eclectic mix to coalesce into a cohesive and intentional display.

Experiment with color harmonies – choose a dominant color and use it in varying intensities throughout the gallery. Alternatively, focus on a theme, such as nature, travel, or abstract expressions, to create a narrative that weaves through the diverse pieces. Finding common threads is about creating visual connections that guide the viewer's eye and invite them to explore the eclectic stories within the gallery.

4. Rule-Breaking Brilliance: Defying Conventions for Impactful Displays:

In the art of mixing and matching, rule-breaking brilliance takes center stage. Don't shy away from defying conventions and challenging traditional norms in your wall gallery. Experiment with asymmetry, unconventional spacing, and varying sizes to create a visually dynamic and impactful display. Allow pieces to overlap or extend beyond the boundaries of a traditional grid, adding an element of spontaneity and energy.

Consider incorporating oversized pieces that become focal points, breaking the mold of uniformity and adding a touch of drama. Mix portrait and landscape orientations for an eclectic visual rhythm. Rule-breaking brilliance is about embracing the freedom to curate a gallery that reflects your personality, creativity, and willingness to defy the ordinary for a truly extraordinary display.

5. Personal Touch: Infusing Your Story into the Eclectic Mix of Wall Art:

The true essence of eclectic wall galleries lies in infusing your personal touch into the mix. Let each piece tell a story – whether it's a framed photograph from a memorable trip, a hand-painted canvas that captures your artistic endeavors, or a vintage find with sentimental value. Infusing your story into the eclectic mix adds authenticity and depth, turning your gallery into a narrative of your life and experiences.

Consider incorporating DIY projects or commissioned artworks that reflect your unique taste and style. Mix in personal memorabilia, such as postcards, letters, or small objects that hold sentimental value. The personal touch transforms your wall gallery from a curated display into a living testament of your journey, making it a source of joy and nostalgia for both you and your visitors.

6. Evolutionary Beauty: Adapting and Refreshing Your Eclectic Wall Gallery:

The beauty of an eclectic wall gallery lies in its ability to evolve and adapt over time. Don't consider it a static arrangement; instead, view it as an ever-changing canvas that can be refreshed and reimagined. Add new pieces that resonate with your current interests, replace artworks that have served their time, or experiment with different layouts to breathe new life into the gallery.

Consider seasonal rotations, where you introduce pieces that reflect the mood or theme of a specific time of year. The evolutionary beauty of your eclectic wall gallery ensures that it remains a dynamic and ever-interesting focal point in your home. Embrace the joy of discovery as you explore new pieces, rearrange existing ones, and let your wall gallery grow and evolve alongside your changing tastes and experiences.

Conclusion:

As we conclude our exploration of the art of mixing and matching for eclectic wall galleries, remember that there are no strict rules – only the canvas of your creativity waiting to be adorned. From the symphony of styles to beyond frames, finding common threads to rule-breaking brilliance, infusing personal touch to evolutionary beauty, the journey is yours to curate. So, let your walls reflect the vibrant tapestry of your eclectic taste, and may your gallery be a testament to the beauty of diversity and creativity.

GLEAMING STATEMENTS: UNVEILING THE ELEGANCE OF METAL WALL ART

Step into a world of sophistication and shine as we explore the captivating allure of metal wall art. In this blog post, we'll dive into the realm of metallic marvels, discovering how the elegance of metal transforms your walls into gleaming statements of artistic expression. From contemporary designs to timeless classics, join us on a journey through the mesmerizing world of metal wall art that elevates the aesthetic appeal of any space.

1. The Alchemy of Metal: Exploring the Diverse Finishes and Textures:

Our first stop is the alchemy of metal, where we explore the vast array of finishes and textures that contribute to the unique charm of metal wall art. Whether it's the sleekness of polished stainless steel, the rustic allure of weathered iron, or the warm glow of brushed bronze, the diverse finishes allow you to tailor your metal art to the specific aesthetic of your space.

Consider experimenting with textures, such as hammered surfaces or laser-cut detailing, to add depth and visual interest to your metal wall art. The alchemy of metal lies in its ability to adapt to various styles – from industrial and modern to rustic and eclectic. Embrace the versatility of metal finishes, and let your walls shimmer with the transformative power of different textures that make each piece a truly individual work of art.

2. Contemporary Statements: Making a Splash with Modern Metal Art:

Venture into the world of contemporary statements, where modern metal art takes center stage in transforming your space into a gallery of cutting-edge design. Picture sleek lines, abstract forms, and geometric shapes that create a visual impact and add a touch of avant-garde sophistication to your walls. Contemporary metal art is a dynamic choice for those looking to make a bold statement in their interior decor.

Consider selecting a large, statement piece that becomes the focal point of a room or create a curated collection of smaller pieces for a gallery effect. The clean lines and minimalist appeal of contemporary metal art make it a perfect match for modern and urban interiors. Make a splash with modern metal art that not only adorns your walls but also becomes a conversation starter, reflecting your keen eye for contemporary aesthetics.

3. Timeless Classics: Nostalgia and Elegance in Vintage Metal Art:

Travel back in time and immerse yourself in the nostalgia and elegance of vintage metal art. Timeless classics in metal wall art often feature intricate scrollwork, ornate details, and vintage-inspired motifs that evoke a sense of old-world charm. These pieces bring a touch of history into your home, creating a harmonious blend of the past and present.

Consider choosing vintage metal art that complements the existing decor of your space, whether it's a Victorian-inspired piece for a touch of romance or an art deco design for a dose of glamour. Vintage metal art transcends trends, offering enduring elegance that stands the test of time. Let your walls become a canvas for timeless classics, infusing your space with the charm and sophistication of bygone eras.

4. Nature's Dance: Bringing the Outdoors In with Botanical Metal Art:

Invite the beauty of nature into your home with the enchanting dance of botanical metal art. Picture walls adorned with delicate metal flowers, leaves, or tree branches that capture the essence of the outdoors. Botanical metal art allows you to bring the serenity and grace of nature indoors, creating a visual symphony that transforms your living space into a blooming garden.

Consider arranging a series of botanical metal pieces to create a cohesive theme, or opt for a statement sculpture that becomes the focal point of a room. The versatility of botanical metal art makes it suitable for various decor styles, from traditional to contemporary. Let your walls bloom with the organic elegance of nature's dance, and watch as your home becomes a haven of natural beauty.

5. Custom Creations: Personalizing Your Space with Bespoke Metal Art:

Enter the realm of custom creations, where metal wall art becomes a canvas for your unique vision and personal style. Many artisans offer bespoke metal art services, allowing you to collaborate on a one-of-a-kind piece that reflects your individuality. Custom metal art adds a personal touch to your space, ensuring that your walls tell a story that is uniquely yours.

Consider working with an artist to create a piece that resonates with your interests, passions, or even incorporates meaningful symbols. Whether it's a personalized metal sculpture, a custom-designed metal sign, or a unique wall installation, custom creations allow you to infuse your space with a sense of identity and purpose. Turn your walls into a showcase of your individuality with bespoke metal art that goes beyond the ordinary.

6. Lighting Elegance: Illuminating Spaces with Metal Wall Sconces:

Conclude our exploration by delving into the elegance of lighting with metal wall sconces. Beyond traditional art, metal extends its charm into functional decor by serving as the material for stylish and sophisticated wall sconces. Picture walls bathed in the soft glow of metal fixtures that not only illuminate your space but also add a touch of glamour and refinement.

Consider choosing metal wall sconces that complement the overall decor theme, whether it's a contemporary design with clean lines or a vintage-inspired piece with ornate details. The play of light and shadow created by metal wall sconces adds depth and ambiance to your space, turning walls into elegant backdrops. Illuminate your home with the timeless elegance of metal wall sconces, and let your walls become a source of both art and light.

Conclusion:

As we conclude our journey through the elegance of metal wall art, remember that the beauty of metal lies not only in its durability and versatility but also in its ability to transform your living space into a gallery of sophistication. Whether you choose the alchemy of different finishes, the contemporary statements of modern art, the timeless classics of vintage pieces, the nature's dance of botanical art, the personalized touch of custom creations, or the lighting elegance of metal wall sconces, let your walls gleam with the brilliance of metallic marvels. Elevate your space with the enduring allure of metal wall art and watch as your walls become a canvas of gleaming statements.

CRAFTING A KALEIDOSCOPE: A FRIENDLY GUIDE TO BUILDING A DIVERSE ART COLLECTION

Embarking on the journey of building an art collection is like curating a colorful tapestry of creativity. This guide takes a friendly approach to exploring various styles and mediums, empowering art enthusiasts to create a collection that reflects the rich diversity of artistic expression.

The Canvas Chronicles: Traditional Painting Styles

In the world of art, the canvas is a storyteller waiting to unfold narratives through diverse painting styles. From the vibrant strokes of Impressionism to the bold geometric patterns of Cubism, this section dives into the colorful chronicles of traditional painting styles. Friendly insights on understanding the artistic movements, recognizing iconic artists, and exploring lesser-known gems pave the way for creating a canvas-rich collection that spans epochs and emotions.

Whether you're drawn to the dreamy landscapes of Romanticism or the dynamic energy of Abstract Expressionism, this section encourages you to embrace the kaleidoscope of possibilities within the realm of traditional painting styles.

Sculpting Dreams: Exploring Three-Dimensional Art

Sculptures add a tangible dimension to art collections, inviting viewers to engage with form, texture, and space. This section delves into the world of three-dimensional art, from classical sculptures that echo the elegance of ancient civilizations to contemporary installations that challenge conventional perceptions. Friendly guidance on understanding sculptural techniques, appreciating the interplay of light and shadow, and discovering sculptors across genres ensures that you sculpt a diverse and captivating collection.

As you explore the realm of sculptures, consider the tactile beauty of materials and the narrative potential within each piece. From marble masterpieces to avant-garde installations, this section encourages you to embrace the dynamic allure of three-dimensional art.

Beyond the Frame: Mixed Media and Collage Creations

Breaking free from the confines of traditional mediums, mixed media and collage art offer a playground of innovation and experimentation. This section explores the vibrant world beyond the frame, where artists blend various materials, textures, and found objects to craft eclectic masterpieces. Friendly tips on understanding the collage process, recognizing mixed media techniques, and discovering emerging artists open the door to a realm where creativity knows no bounds.

As you venture into the world of mixed media, revel in the unexpected combinations and the narratives that unfold when disparate elements converge. This section celebrates the joy of embracing the unconventional and building a collection that resonates with the dynamic spirit of mixed media art.

Printmaking Adventures: The Beauty of Reproduction Techniques

Printmaking, with its myriad of techniques, offers a unique avenue for art enthusiasts to explore both traditional and contemporary expressions. From the detailed precision of etching to the bold graphic statements of screen printing, this section guides you through the printmaking adventures. Friendly insights on understanding printmaking processes, recognizing printmakers' signatures, and exploring limited editions empower you to curate a collection that captures the essence of reproduction techniques.

As you navigate the world of printmaking, appreciate the delicate lines, rich textures, and the nuanced variations that each technique brings. This section celebrates the beauty of printmaking as an accessible and diverse medium for building an art collection.

Lens on Creativity: Photography as an Art Form

Photography has evolved into a powerful art form that captures moments, emotions, and narratives. In this section, we shift our lens to explore the vast realm of photography. Friendly guidance on recognizing photographic styles, understanding the impact of composition, and discovering contemporary photographers encourages you to weave visual stories into your collection. From classic black-and-white portraits to experimental digital compositions, photography offers a versatile and dynamic addition to a diverse art collection.

As you delve into the world of photography, consider the narratives embedded in each image and the unique perspectives that photographers bring to their craft. This section celebrates the power of photography to freeze moments in time and enrich your collection with visual narratives.

The Digital Palette: Exploring New Media and Digital Art

In the age of technological innovation, art extends beyond traditional mediums into the digital realm. This section embraces the digital palette, exploring new media and digital art forms. Friendly insights on understanding digital techniques, recognizing influential digital artists, and navigating the evolving landscape of virtual art spaces empower you to incorporate cutting-edge creativity into your collection.

From immersive virtual reality experiences to interactive digital installations, this section encourages you to push the boundaries of your art collection. Embrace the digital frontier, where pixels become brushstrokes, and technology merges seamlessly with artistic expression.

WHITEWASHED BRICK AND ART: INDUSTRIAL CHIC FOR MODERN HOMES

Step into the realm of "Whitewashed Brick and Art," where industrial chic meets modern elegance in perfect harmony. In this blog post, we'll explore the seamless integration of whitewashed brick walls with art, transforming your living spaces into stylish and contemporary sanctuaries. Join us on a journey through six captivating sections, each unveiling the unique charm and design possibilities of this urban-inspired aesthetic.

The Allure of Whitewashed Brick: A Modern Industrial Canvas

In "The Allure of Whitewashed Brick," we delve into the timeless appeal of exposed brick walls and their transformative effect on interior design. Discover how whitewashing adds a contemporary twist, softening the raw industrial vibe while maintaining the texture and character of the bricks. This section sets the stage for the perfect canvas to showcase art in an urban-chic setting.

Consider incorporating whitewashed brick walls in your living room or bedroom to create a modern backdrop that complements various decor styles, from minimalist to eclectic.

Industrial Elegance: The Marriage of Texture and Art

In "Industrial Elegance," we explore how the juxtaposition of textured whitewashed brick with carefully selected art pieces creates a harmonious blend of industrial elegance. Learn how the rough, tactile quality of brickwork enhances the visual interest of art, adding depth and character to your space.

Consider opting for large, statement art pieces that contrast with the subtle texture of whitewashed brick, creating a focal point that draws the eye and elevates the overall aesthetic. Industrial Elegance encourages you to embrace the marriage of texture and art for a truly sophisticated ambiance.

Gallery Wall on Brick: A Curated Urban Showcase

In "Gallery Wall on Brick," we delve into the art of creating curated displays on whitewashed brick surfaces. Explore the dynamic possibilities of arranging diverse art pieces, from framed photographs to abstract paintings, in a gallery-style layout. Learn how the irregularity of brick patterns can enhance the eclectic charm of a well-curated gallery wall.

Consider experimenting with different frame styles and sizes to achieve a visually compelling arrangement that complements the industrial chic vibe. Gallery Wall on Brick invites you to transform your whitewashed brick wall into a curated urban showcase that tells your unique story.

Monochromatic Magic: Black and White Art on Whitewashed Brick

In "Monochromatic Magic," we explore the timeless elegance of black and white art against whitewashed brick backgrounds. Discover how the stark contrast between dark and light elements creates a visually striking effect, emphasizing the beauty of simplicity. Explore the versatility of this color scheme in achieving a contemporary and cohesive look.

Consider incorporating black and white photography or abstract art to achieve monochromatic magic that adds a touch of sophistication to your industrial-chic space. This section encourages you to embrace the power of contrast for a captivating visual impact.

Botanical Oasis: Introducing Nature to Urban Spaces

In "Botanical Oasis," we celebrate the synergy between whitewashed brick walls and nature-inspired art. Explore how botanical prints, plant-themed canvases, and greenery-infused art bring a refreshing touch of nature to urban interiors. Discover the transformative effect of introducing organic elements that soften the industrial backdrop.

Consider creating a botanical oasis with art featuring lush greenery, flowers, and natural motifs, creating a harmonious balance between the urban and the organic. Botanical Oasis invites you to reconnect with nature within the confines of your modern home.

DIY Wall Art on Whitewashed Brick: Personalized Industrial Creativity

In "DIY Wall Art on Whitewashed Brick," we encourage you to unleash your creativity and personalize your industrial chic haven. Discover innovative and budget-friendly DIY art projects that complement the rugged charm of whitewashed brick. From hand-painted canvases to repurposed materials, this section empowers you to infuse your personality into your home decor.

Consider involving family members or friends in a weekend DIY project to create unique art pieces that reflect your individual style. DIY Wall Art on Whitewashed Brick invites you to make your mark on the canvas of your industrial-inspired abode.

Conclusion:

As we conclude our exploration of "Whitewashed Brick and Art," revel in the endless possibilities of creating a modern sanctuary that seamlessly blends industrial chic with artistic expression. Whether you're drawn to the allure of whitewashed brick, industrial elegance, gallery walls, monochromatic magic, botanical oasis, or DIY creativity, each section unveils a facet of this captivating design trend.

EFFORTLESS ELEGANCE: ELEVATING SIMPLE INTERIOR DESIGNS WITH MINIMALIST WALL ART

Welcome to the world of effortless elegance, where the simplicity of minimalist interior design meets the transformative power of wall art. In this blog post, we'll explore the art of infusing minimalist chic into your living space using carefully curated wall art. From understanding the principles of minimalism to selecting the perfect pieces, join us on a journey of creating a harmonious balance between simplicity and sophistication in your home.

1. The Essence of Minimalism: A Primer on Simple Interior Designs:

At the heart of minimalist chic lies the essence of minimalism – a design philosophy that embraces simplicity, functionality, and a sense of calm. Minimalist interiors are characterized by clean lines, a neutral color palette, and a focus on essential elements. In this section, we'll delve into the principles of minimalism, exploring how the absence of excess creates a serene and uncluttered atmosphere.

To achieve a minimalist interior, start by decluttering and paring down unnecessary items. Opt for furniture with clean and simple lines, choosing quality over quantity. The color palette should be neutral, with whites, grays, and earth tones dominating the space. The essence of minimalism is about creating an environment that allows for clarity and focus, setting the perfect stage for the introduction of wall art that complements and enhances the simplicity.

2. The Art of Selecting Minimalist Wall Art: Elevating Simplicity with Sophistication:

In the art of selecting minimalist wall art, the goal is to elevate simplicity with sophistication. Choose pieces that align with the clean lines and neutral palette of minimalist interiors. Consider abstract paintings with uncomplicated compositions, black and white photography that captures the essence of simplicity, or geometric prints that complement the straightforward design of the space.

Opt for large, statement pieces that become focal points without overwhelming the room. A single, well-chosen artwork can speak volumes in a minimalist setting, creating a sense of purpose and intrigue. The art of selecting minimalist wall art is about curating a collection that adds depth and personality without disrupting the serene simplicity of the interior.

3. Negative Space Brilliance: Utilizing Empty Walls for Maximum Impact:

One of the key features of minimalist design is the emphasis on negative space – the unoccupied areas that allow the eye to rest and the mind to appreciate simplicity. In this section, we'll explore the brilliance of utilizing empty walls for maximum impact. Consider leaving large sections of walls bare, allowing the negative space to become a design element in itself.

Introduce wall art strategically, ensuring it complements rather than competes with the negative space. A single piece placed on an empty wall can become a focal point, drawing attention without cluttering the visual landscape. Negative space brilliance is about appreciating the beauty of simplicity and restraint, creating a sense of openness and calm within the living space.

4. Monochromatic Magic: Infusing Depth with a Limited Color Palette:

In minimalist chic, monochromatic magic becomes a powerful tool for infusing depth into the interior design. Embrace a limited color palette, focusing on shades of a single color or subtle variations of neutrals. In this section, we'll explore how a monochromatic approach enhances the minimalist aesthetic and sets the stage for wall art that seamlessly integrates into the design.

Choose wall art that aligns with the selected color scheme, whether it's a grayscale photograph, a single-color abstract painting, or a monochromatic print. The magic of monochromatic design lies in its ability to create a cohesive and harmonious atmosphere. The limited color palette allows for subtle variations in texture, form, and shade to shine through, adding sophistication and visual interest to the simplicity of the interior.

5. Functional Art: Blurring the Line Between Form and Purpose:

Minimalist chic celebrates the marriage of form and purpose, and in this section, we'll explore the concept of functional art. Choose wall art that goes beyond mere decoration and serves a purpose within the space. This could be a wall-mounted shelf with integrated art, a minimalist clock that doubles as a design statement, or a series of framed botanical prints that bring a touch of nature indoors.

Functional art blurs the line between form and purpose, enhancing the practicality of minimalist interiors. Consider incorporating wall-mounted storage units that also showcase decorative elements, or mirrors that serve both a functional and aesthetic role. The beauty of functional art lies in its ability to contribute to the overall design while maintaining the simplicity and purposeful nature of minimalist chic.

6. Evolutionary Simplicity: Adapting and Refreshing Minimalist Interior Designs:

Minimalist chic is not about stagnancy; it's about the beauty of evolutionary simplicity. In this final section, we'll explore the concept of adapting and refreshing minimalist interior designs over time. While the core principles of minimalism remain, the living space can evolve with the introduction of new wall art, rearrangements, or subtle shifts in color palettes.

Consider seasonal updates, where wall art reflects the changing colors and moods of different times of the year. Embrace the joy of discovering new minimalist pieces that resonate with your evolving taste. The evolutionary simplicity of minimalist interior designs ensures that the living space remains dynamic and harmonious, offering a canvas for continual refinement and personalization.

Conclusion:

As we conclude our exploration of minimalist chic and the art of using wall art in simple interior designs, remember that elegance lies in the balance between simplicity and sophistication. From understanding the essence of minimalism to selecting the perfect pieces, utilizing negative space to embracing monochromatic magic, and exploring functional art to the concept of evolutionary simplicity – let your living space be a canvas of refined simplicity, where every wall art piece contributes to the harmonious and purposeful atmosphere.

NATURE'S SYMPHONY: INFUSING LIFE WITH EARTHY TONES AND ART

Step into a world where the vibrant hues of nature come alive within the walls of your home. In this blog post, we'll explore the enchanting realm of earthy tones and art – a combination that transcends mere decoration, creating a haven that echoes the beauty of the great outdoors. From the tranquility of natural hues to the artistic expressions that mimic the wonders of the earth, join us on a journey of bringing nature's palette indoors and transforming your living space into a harmonious sanctuary.

1. The Alchemy of Earthy Tones: Bringing Nature's Palette Indoors:

Nature's palette is a rich tapestry of earthy tones that captivate the senses and create a sense of grounding. Embracing these tones within your home is like inviting the spirit of the outdoors to dance through your living space. The alchemy begins with colors like warm browns, calming greens, and serene blues – shades that echo the natural beauty of landscapes, forests, and oceans.

Transitioning your home to earthy tones is a visual and sensory experience. Imagine the comfort of stepping onto a plush rug in a shade reminiscent of sun-drenched sand or the serenity of a bedroom adorned in the calming hues of a misty forest. These earthy tones create a seamless connection between the indoors and the outdoors, fostering a sense of tranquility and relaxation.

2. Art in Earthy Tones for Natural and Organic Home Decor:

The marriage of art and earthy tones brings forth a symphony of natural and organic home decor. Artworks in these tones become not just decorative elements but storytellers that echo the essence of the earth. Consider investing in paintings or prints that depict landscapes, botanicals, or abstract interpretations of nature. These pieces serve as windows to the outdoors, creating a connection with the natural world within the confines of your home.

Art in earthy tones also allows you to experiment with textures and mediums that enhance the organic feel. Canvas prints that mimic the grain of wood, sculptures inspired by the forms of rocks, or abstract artworks that capture the fluidity of water – the choices are as diverse as nature itself. Each piece becomes a focal point, a statement that celebrates the beauty of simplicity and the elegance of the earth's color palette.

3. Using Earthy Colors in Wall Art to Evoke Nature's Beauty Indoors:

The walls of your home are a canvas waiting to be adorned with the breathtaking beauty of nature's hues. Using earthy colors in wall art is a transformative experience that evokes the essence of the great outdoors. Whether it's a large canvas depicting a sun-kissed desert landscape or a series of smaller prints showcasing the intricate details of leaves and branches, the goal is to bring the soul-soothing charm of nature into your living space.

Consider creating a gallery wall with a curated collection of artworks in earthy tones. This arrangement can tell a visual story, mirroring the diversity found in the natural world. Experiment with different frames or opt for a frameless look to enhance the organic feel. The walls become a living tapestry, an ever-changing reflection of the seasons and the beauty that nature unfurls.

4. Nature's Serenity in Earthy Bedrooms: Creating a Tranquil Oasis:

Your bedroom is a sanctuary, a place where you retreat to find peace and rejuvenate your spirit. Infusing earthy tones and art into your bedroom creates a tranquil oasis that embraces the serenity of nature. Choose bedding and linens in calming shades, complemented by artworks that echo the gentle whispers of the outdoors – perhaps a moonlit forest or a misty mountain sunrise.

The furniture in your bedroom can also contribute to the earthy theme. Opt for natural wood finishes that enhance the organic ambiance. Consider adding elements like indoor plants to breathe life into the space. The result is a bedroom that becomes a cocoon of tranquility, inviting you to unwind, relax, and connect with the natural rhythms that earthy tones evoke.

5. Earthy Tones in the Kitchen: Infusing Warmth and Rustic Charm:

The kitchen, often considered the heart of the home, can also benefit from the warmth and rustic charm of earthy tones. Consider incorporating these colors into your kitchen through art, decor, and even culinary elements. Artworks depicting farm landscapes, herb gardens, or rustic kitchen scenes can infuse a sense of authenticity and natural beauty.

To enhance the earthy ambiance, opt for kitchenware and utensils in warm tones, like terracotta pots, wooden cutting boards, or copper cookware. Open shelving allows you to showcase these elements, turning functional items into decorative pieces. The earthy tones in your kitchen create a welcoming atmosphere, making it a space not just for cooking but for savoring the simple joys of life.

6. Seasonal Transitions: Adapting Earthy Tones to the Changing Landscape:

Nature is a master of seasonal transformations, and your home can echo this rhythm by adapting earthy tones to the changing landscape outside your window. Consider updating your decor and artworks with the seasons – warm, golden hues in autumn, cool blues and greens for spring, and crisp whites and greys for winter. This seasonal transition not only keeps your living space fresh but also connects you to the ever-changing beauty of the natural world.

Adapting earthy tones to the seasons doesn't mean a complete overhaul of your decor; subtle changes can make a significant impact. Swap out throw pillows, change the artwork on the walls, or introduce seasonal flowers and foliage. This dynamic approach ensures that your home remains a living canvas, mirroring the ebb and flow of nature's color palette.

Conclusion:

As we conclude our exploration into the world of earthy tones and art, remember that the magic lies in the connection between your living space and the great outdoors. The earthy palette becomes a bridge, bringing nature's tranquility, beauty, and simplicity into the heart of your home. From the walls adorned with nature-inspired artworks to the serenity of your bedroom and the warmth of your kitchen, infusing earthy tones is a transformative journey that creates a harmonious haven where you can find solace and inspiration.

UNVEILING THE CANVAS: A BEGINNER'S GUIDE TO ART COLLECTING

ART COLLECTING TIPS FOR BEGINNERS

EMBARKING ON THE ARTISTIC JOURNEY

Art collecting is more than just a hobby; it's a journey into the diverse and fascinating world of creativity. As a beginner, you stand at the threshold of an enriching experience. Start by exploring different art forms, understanding your preferences, and gradually developing your unique taste.

Navigating the Art Market

Dive into the vibrant art market with confidence. Learn about various platforms, from galleries to online marketplaces. Understanding the dynamics of pricing, artist reputations, and market trends will empower you to make informed choices.

The Art of Budgeting

Art collecting doesn't have to break the bank. Establishing a budget helps you navigate the vast art landscape without compromising your financial well-being. Discover affordable yet promising artists and gradually build your collection over time.

Cultivating Your Artistic Eye

Developing an artistic eye is a skill that evolves over time. Train yourself to appreciate different styles, techniques, and genres. Attend exhibitions, visit galleries, and engage in conversations with artists to refine your understanding of art.

The Personal Connection: Choosing Art That Speaks to You

Your collection is an extension of your personality. Select pieces that resonate with you on a personal level. Whether it's a painting, sculpture, or digital art, the emotional connection you feel is what makes your collection truly yours.

Demystifying the Artwork Description

Understanding the context and story behind each artwork enhances your appreciation. Dive into the artist's background, the inspiration behind the piece, and the techniques employed. This knowledge transforms a mere object into a narrative waiting to be explored.

Conservation and Care

Preserving your art collection is an essential aspect of art collecting. Learn about proper handling, framing, and environmental considerations to ensure your pieces stand the test of time.

Networking with the Art Community

Immerse yourself in the vibrant art community. Attend events, join forums, and connect with fellow collectors, artists, and enthusiasts. Networking not only enriches your knowledge but opens doors to new opportunities and collaborations.

Beyond the Walls: Exploring Art Beyond Traditional Formats

Art extends beyond canvas and frames. Explore unconventional forms like digital art, installations, and mixed media. Embracing diversity adds a dynamic flair to your collection.

The Power of Patience

Building a meaningful art collection takes time. Be patient, allowing your tastes and preferences to evolve naturally. Embrace the journey, enjoying the process of discovering, acquiring, and cherishing each piece.

Showcasing Your Collection: Creating a Home Gallery

Transform your living space into a curated haven for your collection. Learn the art of displaying pieces to enhance their visual impact and create a harmonious ensemble.

Supporting Emerging Artists

Contribute to the art ecosystem by supporting emerging talents. Not only does this provide exposure for new artists, but it also adds an element of discovery and freshness to your collection.

Curating Themes: Building Cohesion in Your Collection

Create thematic threads within your collection. Whether it's a particular art movement, color palette, or conceptual focus, curating themes adds depth and coherence to your evolving gallery.

Balancing Trends and Timelessness

While staying attuned to contemporary art trends is exciting, don't shy away from timeless classics. Striking a balance between the two ensures your collection remains relevant and enduring.

The Thrill of the Auction: Participating Wisely

Participating in art auctions can be exhilarating. Equip yourself with knowledge about the auction process, set realistic bidding limits, and relish the excitement of acquiring coveted pieces.

Reflection and Evolution: Your Artistic Legacy

As your collection grows, take moments to reflect on its evolution. Your art collection is a living testament to your journey, passions, and the ever-evolving landscape of the art world.

ARTFUL SEASONS: TRANSFORMING YOUR SPACE WITH ROTATING WALL ART TO REFLECT THE TIME OF YEAR

Welcome to the ever-changing canvas of your home, where the seasons unfold in a symphony of colors and themes. In this blog post, we'll explore the delightful practice of rotating wall art to reflect the time of year, infusing your living space with the spirit of each season. From the warmth of autumn hues to the freshness of spring florals, join us on a journey of artful seasons that transforms your home into a dynamic and ever-evolving gallery.

Autumnal Aura: Cozying Up with Warm Hues and Nature-Inspired Art

As the leaves outside begin to change, let your walls embrace the autumnal aura with a rotation of wall art that mirrors the warmth and coziness of the season. Consider swapping out bright and airy pieces for artworks featuring rich, earthy tones like deep reds, burnt oranges, and golden yellows. Nature-inspired art, showcasing fall foliage, pumpkins, and cozy scenes, creates a seamless connection with the changing landscape outside.

Capture the essence of fall with framed prints, canvases, or even seasonal wall hangings that evoke the crisp air and the scent of fallen leaves. This rotation not only brings a touch of autumnal charm into your home but also ensures that your space remains in harmony with the outside world, creating a sense of continuity and connection with the season.

Winter Whimsy: Embracing the Magic of Snowy Scenes and Festive Art

As winter blankets the world in a layer of snow, let your walls embrace the enchanting charm of the season with a rotation of art that reflects winter whimsy. Swap out autumnal tones for cool blues, silvers, and whites that capture the serene beauty of snowy landscapes. Consider featuring winter-themed art, such as snow-covered trees, festive holiday scenes, or whimsical snowflakes, to infuse your space with a touch of magic.

Integrate seasonal elements like cozy knitted textures in wall hangings or metallic accents that mimic the glimmer of frost. Rotating wall art for winter not only elevates the festive ambiance but also allows you to create a cozy and inviting atmosphere that resonates with the spirit of the season. Embrace the magic of winter with art that brings the beauty of snow and the warmth of holiday celebrations into your home.

Springtime Bloom: Infusing Your Space with Floral Delights and Pastel Hues

As the world awakens from its winter slumber, invite the freshness and vibrancy of spring into your home with a rotation of wall art that mirrors the bloom outside. Replace winter whites with a palette of pastel hues, featuring soft pinks, greens, and blues that capture the essence of new beginnings. Infuse your space with floral delights, whether it's botanical prints, watercolor blossoms, or vibrant images of spring gardens in full bloom.

Consider incorporating nature-inspired textures like woven baskets or floral wreaths as complementary elements. The rotation for spring should evoke a sense of renewal and energy, transforming your home into a sanctuary that mirrors the awakening world outside. Embrace the blooming beauty of spring with wall art that celebrates the arrival of warmer days and the promise of new growth.

Summer Serenity: Embracing Sun-Kissed Vibes and Coastal Art

As the days lengthen and the sun bathes everything in a golden glow, rotate your wall art to embrace the serene vibes of summer. Swap out the pastel hues for brighter, sun-kissed tones that capture the essence of the season. Integrate coastal and beach-themed art to evoke the relaxed and carefree atmosphere of summer days spent by the shore.

Consider incorporating natural textures like woven seagrass or light linen fabrics to enhance the coastal theme. The rotation for summer should create a sense of tranquility and relaxation, turning your home into a retreat that mirrors the easygoing vibes of the season. Embrace the serenity of summer with wall art that transports you to sun-drenched beaches and lazy afternoons.

Holiday Cheer: Festive Rotations for Celebratory Seasons

Celebrate the joyous occasions and festive holidays with a rotation of wall art that reflects the unique cheer of these special seasons. Whether it's Christmas, Hanukkah, Diwali, or any other festive celebration, infuse your space with the spirit of the occasion. Swap out everyday art for holiday-themed pieces that showcase traditional symbols, colors, and motifs associated with the festivities.

Consider integrating festive decor elements like twinkling lights, garlands, or seasonal ornaments that complement the holiday-themed artwork. The rotation for celebratory seasons not only adds a touch of merriment to your home but also creates a dynamic and ever-changing environment that evolves with each joyous occasion. Embrace the holiday cheer with wall art that transforms your space into a festive haven during these special times.

Transitional Touches: Seamlessly Navigating Between Seasons

As seasons transition, consider incorporating transitional touches into your rotation strategy to seamlessly navigate between different times of the year. Opt for versatile artworks that complement multiple seasons, featuring neutral color palettes or nature-inspired themes that transcend the specific characteristics of each season.

Consider rotating art that captures the essence of transitional periods, like the changing leaves of autumn or the blossoming buds of spring. This approach allows your home to transition smoothly between seasons, creating a sense of continuity and flow. Embrace the artful practice of transitional touches to maintain a dynamic yet cohesive aesthetic in your living space throughout the year.

Conclusion:

In conclusion, the artful practice of rotating wall art to reflect the time of year transforms your home into a dynamic canvas that evolves with the changing seasons. From the autumnal aura to winter whimsy, springtime bloom, summer serenity, holiday cheer, and transitional touches, each rotation adds a layer of charm and continuity to your living space. Embrace the ever-changing canvas of your home, where art and seasons dance together, creating a space that resonates with the beauty of each passing season.

PIXEL PERFECTION: THE FUSION OF ART AND TECHNOLOGY WITH DIGITAL ART DISPLAYS

Welcome to the future of home décor, where art meets technology in a symphony of pixels and possibilities. In this blog post, we'll explore the transformative world of Digital Art Displays, unraveling the ways in which technology seamlessly integrates with home décor. From dynamic displays that evolve with your mood to interactive pieces that respond to your touch, join us on a journey into the pixelated realm where the boundaries between art and technology blur, creating a visually stunning and technologically advanced living space.

The Art of Pixels: Unveiling the Beauty of Digital Art

Begin our exploration in the first section, "The Art of Pixels," where we delve into the visual allure of digital art. Unlike traditional forms, digital art allows for an intricate dance of pixels, creating visuals that are both crisp and captivating. Explore the limitless possibilities of color, motion, and form as digital artists craft masterpieces that come to life on your screens.

Consider the mesmerizing works of artists like Beeple or Refik Anadol, whose digital creations push the boundaries of what's possible. Digital art displays bring these pixel-perfect creations into your home, transforming your walls into dynamic canvases that evolve with the touch of a button. Immerse yourself in the world of pixels, where every brushstroke is a pixel and every pixel tells a story.

Dynamic Décor: Changing Moods with Digital Art Displays

Move on to the second section, "Dynamic Décor," where we explore how digital art displays have the power to change the mood of your space in an instant. One moment, your living room is bathed in the warm hues of a sunset, and the next, it transforms into a vibrant cityscape alive with energy. Digital art displays offer a level of versatility that goes beyond static pieces, allowing you to curate the ambiance of your home with a simple tap.

Consider incorporating digital displays that sync with the time of day or your current activity, creating an immersive experience that adapts to your lifestyle. Whether it's a tranquil seascape during relaxation or an energizing abstract pattern for productivity, dynamic décor turns your home into a living canvas that reflects the ebb and flow of your day.

Interactive Experiences: Touch, Swipe, and Engage

Enter the third section, "Interactive Experiences," where we unravel the magic of touch, swipe, and engage. Unlike traditional art, digital displays invite interaction, turning your living space into an immersive experience. Imagine a wall that responds to your touch, allowing you to explore different layers of a digital masterpiece or even create your own art with a virtual palette.

Consider artists like Daniel Rozin, whose interactive installations mirror your movements in real-time, creating a dynamic dialogue between viewer and art. Incorporating interactive experiences into your home décor not only adds an element of playfulness but also fosters a deeper connection with the art. Dive into the world of touch-sensitive pixels and discover how your walls can respond to the gentlest caress.

Smart Integration: Syncing Digital Art with Home Automation

In the fourth section, "Smart Integration," we explore the seamless syncing of digital art with home automation. Imagine a home where your digital art display becomes an integral part of your smart ecosystem, adjusting its visuals based on your preferences, time of day, or even the weather outside. Smart integration takes your digital art to the next level, creating a holistic and connected living experience.

Explore how platforms like Samsung's The Frame or LG's OLED Gallery TVs seamlessly integrate with smart home systems, allowing you to control your art with voice commands or automated routines. As technology continues to evolve, so does the synergy between digital art and smart living, making your home a hub of interconnected creativity.

Virtual Galleries: Curating Art Collections in the Digital Realm

Move on to the fifth section, "Virtual Galleries," where we explore the concept of curating art collections in the digital realm. Digital art displays open the door to virtual galleries that transcend physical constraints, allowing you to curate an ever-evolving collection of masterpieces. Explore works from renowned artists or discover emerging talents without the limitations of wall space or storage.

Consider the possibilities of creating themed galleries that change with the seasons or rotating curated collections that align with your mood. Virtual galleries bring the world of art to your fingertips, allowing you to curate an eclectic and ever-changing exhibition within the confines of your home. Step into the future of curation where every room becomes a curated gallery space.

Customization Unleashed: Tailoring Digital Art to Your Aesthetic

In the final section, "Customization Unleashed," we unravel the power of tailoring digital art to your aesthetic. Digital displays offer unprecedented customization options, allowing you to upload your own images, animations, or even collaborate with digital artists to create pieces that resonate with your unique taste.

Consider creating a digital art display that complements your interior design or serves as a focal point in a minimalist space. With customization options ranging from color schemes to motion preferences, your digital art becomes a true reflection of your aesthetic sensibilities. Embrace the freedom to unleash your creativity on the digital canvas and discover the joy of living with art that is as unique as you are.

Conclusion:

As we conclude our journey through the pixelated wonderland of Digital Art Displays, remember that the fusion of art and technology opens new dimensions in home décor. From the art of pixels and dynamic décor to interactive experiences, smart integration, virtual galleries, and customization unleashed, each section has unveiled a facet of the transformative power that digital art brings to your living space. Embrace the future where pixels become paintbrushes, and your walls become a canvas of endless possibilities.

BLANK CANVAS BRILLIANCE: FROM BLANK WALLS TO HIGH VALUE - ARTISTIC HOME TRANSFORMATIONS

Setting the Stage for Artistic Home Transformations

Welcome to a journey of blank canvas brilliance where we unravel the secrets of turning empty walls into high-value artistic showcases. In this guide, we explore the transformative power of art in your home, showcasing how strategic choices and creative flair can elevate your living spaces. Get ready to be inspired as we delve into the world of artistic home transformations, proving that every blank wall is an opportunity waiting to be seized.

"The Power of a Pinnacle Piece: Making a Statement with a Focal Point"

In "The Power of a Pinnacle Piece," we explore the impact of a statement artwork, a pinnacle piece that sets the tone for the entire space. Learn how a carefully chosen painting, sculpture, or unique art installation can turn a blank wall into a captivating focal point. Discover the art of selecting pieces that not only resonate with your style but also add substantial value to your home, creating a lasting impression that elevates its overall aesthetic.

Unlock the secrets of making a bold statement with your pinnacle piece, transforming your blank canvas into a high-value masterpiece.

"Gallery Elegance: Creating Sophistication with Curated Art Collections"

In "Gallery Elegance," we delve into the world of curated art collections, demonstrating how a carefully arranged ensemble of artworks can elevate the sophistication of your home. Explore the art of mixing and matching different styles, sizes, and mediums to create a gallery-like experience within your own living space. Learn how a well-curated collection adds depth, character, and an air of sophistication to your walls, turning a blank canvas into a gallery of your personal taste and style.

Discover the magic of gallery elegance and witness your home's transformation into a refined and curated masterpiece.

"Nature's Embrace: Infusing Tranquility with Botanical and Landscape Art"

In "Nature's Embrace," we turn to the tranquility of nature, exploring how botanical and landscape art can infuse your home with a sense of calm and serenity. Dive into the world of natural motifs, whether it's a stunning landscape painting or a collection of botanical prints. Learn how these elements can turn your blank walls into serene retreats, enhancing the overall value of your home by creating an environment that speaks to the beauty of the outdoors.

Embark on a journey of nature's embrace and witness the transformation of your home into a tranquil haven.

"The Personal Touch: Custom and Personalized Art for Value Enhancement"

In "The Personal Touch," we celebrate the uniqueness of custom and personalized art, demonstrating how these pieces can add significant value to your home. Explore the world of commissioned artworks, family portraits, or personalized installations that tell your story. Learn how incorporating elements of your life and personality into your home's decor not only adds sentimental value but also enhances its market value by making it stand out in a sea of generic designs.

Uncover the magic of the personal touch and witness your home's transformation into a uniquely valuable space.

"Dynamic Duos: Pairing Art with Architecture for Seamless Integration"

In "Dynamic Duos," we explore the synergy between art and architecture, showcasing how these dynamic duos can seamlessly integrate to elevate your home's aesthetic. Learn how to strategically pair artworks with architectural elements to create a cohesive design that enhances the overall appeal of your living spaces. Dive into the art of blending form and function, turning your blank walls into integrated masterpieces that not only complement but also amplify the architectural features of your home.

Discover the transformative power of dynamic duos and witness your home's architectural elements come to life in harmony with art.

"Art-Tech Fusion: Elevating Homes with Innovative Technological Installations"

In "Art-Tech Fusion," we embrace the future by exploring how technological installations can be seamlessly integrated into your home's artistic transformation. From interactive displays to digital art installations, learn how technology can add a contemporary and innovative edge to your living spaces. Dive into the world of art-tech fusion, witnessing the convergence of creativity and technology to turn your home into a cutting-edge, high-value masterpiece.

Explore the limitless possibilities of art-tech fusion and see your home's transformation into a technologically advanced work of art.

ARTFUL HARMONY: A GUIDE TO CHOOSING THE PERFECT WALL ART FOR YOUR LIVING ROOM

Welcome to the canvas of your living room, where the walls await an infusion of personality and style. In this blog post, we'll embark on a journey to discover the art of choosing the perfect wall art for your living space. From understanding the nuances of living room aesthetics to practical tips for selecting the ideal pieces, let's explore how art can become the soulful heartbeat of your home, reflecting your taste, evoking emotions, and transforming your living room into a curated masterpiece.

1. The Living Room Canvas: Decoding the Art of Choosing Wall Art:

Your living room is the heart of your home, and the wall art you choose sets the tone for the entire space. Decoding the art of choosing wall art begins with understanding the canvas of your living room – the color scheme, the furniture, the lighting, and the overall ambiance. Consider the existing aesthetic and theme; whether it's modern, rustic, eclectic, or minimalist, the art you choose should harmonize with the existing elements, creating a cohesive and visually appealing ensemble.

Think about the emotions you want the living room to evoke. Do you aim for a serene and tranquil space or one that exudes energy and vibrancy? The living room canvas is your palette; let your art be the brushstroke that tells the story. Whether you opt for a single large piece as a focal point or a curated gallery wall that weaves together a tapestry of memories, the key is to choose wall art that complements the living room's essence.

2. Selecting the Perfect Living Room Wall Decor:

The quest for the perfect living room wall decor is a delightful adventure into the realms of style, personality, and artistic expression. Begin by considering the size and scale of your walls. A large living room can accommodate oversized artworks or a gallery wall, while smaller spaces may benefit from a well-chosen statement piece. Balance is key – avoid overwhelming the space with art that is too large or making it feel bare with pieces that are too small.

Experiment with different mediums and styles to find the perfect living room wall decor. Consider framed prints for a classic and polished look, canvas prints for texture and depth, or even three-dimensional art for added visual interest. The living room is a canvas for your creativity, so don't be afraid to mix and match different pieces that resonate with your taste and create a dynamic and visually appealing display.

3. Tips for Finding the Ideal Art for Your Living Space:

Finding the ideal art for your living space involves a blend of intuition, personal taste, and a few practical considerations. Start by identifying a theme or color scheme that resonates with you. Whether it's nature-inspired art, abstract expressions, or a collection of family photos, having a theme can guide your choices and create a cohesive look.

Consider the furniture and layout of your living room. The art you choose should complement the overall design and not compete for attention. Pay attention to the color palette – harmonize or contrast, depending on the desired effect. If your living room has neutral tones, art can become the vibrant accent that injects personality. Conversely, in a colorful room, art with more subdued hues can provide balance.

4. Creating Visual Flow: Arranging Wall Art for a Harmonious Display:

Once you've selected the perfect pieces, the next step is arranging wall art for a harmonious display. Creating visual flow involves considering the layout, spacing, and proportions of the art on your walls. A gallery wall can be a stunning choice, allowing you to showcase a collection of artworks that tell a visual story. Experiment with different arrangements before committing to a final layout.

Consider the height at which you hang your art; eye level is a good rule of thumb for optimal viewing. For larger pieces, leave enough space around them to allow the art to breathe. If you have a collection of smaller pieces, play with asymmetry and varied spacing to create a dynamic and visually interesting arrangement. The goal is to create a sense of unity and flow, where each piece complements the others, and the display feels curated rather than cluttered.

5. Infusing Personality: Customizing Wall Art to Reflect Your Style:

The beauty of choosing wall art for your living room lies in its ability to infuse personality into the space. Don't hesitate to customize pieces to reflect your unique style and preferences. Consider commissioned artwork that captures your vision or personal photographs that hold sentimental value. Adding a touch of personality to your living room wall art ensures that the space feels authentically yours.

Experiment with DIY projects or explore local artists who can create custom pieces tailored to your taste. The living room is a reflection of your lifestyle, hobbies, and interests, and the art you choose should amplify these aspects. Whether it's a vintage map representing your love for travel or an abstract painting inspired by your favorite colors, customization adds a layer of intimacy to your living space.

6. Seasonal Refresh: Adapting Wall Art to Changing Tastes and Trends:

As the seasons change, so do your tastes and the trends in interior design. Consider a seasonal refresh for your living room wall art, allowing you to experiment with different themes, colors, and styles. This doesn't mean a complete overhaul; small changes can make a significant impact. Swap out a few pieces, introduce new artworks that reflect the current season, or even consider rotating artworks from other rooms.

Adapting wall art to changing tastes and trends ensures that your living room remains dynamic and reflects your evolving aesthetic. It's an opportunity to explore new artists, embrace emerging trends, or even rediscover forgotten pieces in your collection. The seasonal refresh keeps your living room wall art exciting and ever-evolving, making the space feel continuously curated and infused with freshness.

Conclusion:

Choosing the perfect wall art for your living room is a journey of self-expression, creativity, and thoughtful curation. The living room becomes a canvas waiting to be adorned with pieces that tell your story, evoke emotions, and transform the space into a haven of personal style. From understanding the living room canvas to creating visual flow and infusing personality, the artful harmony of choosing wall art ensures that your living space becomes a curated masterpiece that resonates with your unique taste.

GOLDEN ELEGANCE: TRANSFORMING YOUR SPACE WITH GLAMOROUS METALLIC ACCENTS

Prepare to immerse yourself in the opulent world of golden elegance as we explore the transformative power of metallic accents in home decor. In this blog post, "Golden Elegance," we'll delve into the allure of gold and other metallic finishes, uncovering the art of elevating your living space with a touch of glamour. From shimmering gold leaf to sleek silver and bronze, discover how metallic accents can add sophistication, warmth, and a touch of luxury to your decor.

Gilded Grandeur: The Timeless Allure of Gold

Embark on our journey with "Gilded Grandeur," where we explore the timeless allure of gold in home decor. Gold has long been associated with luxury, wealth, and timeless sophistication. Whether it's in the form of gilded frames, gold leaf accents on furniture, or metallic wall art, the introduction of gold instantly elevates the ambiance of any space.

Consider incorporating gold accents in unexpected places, such as lighting fixtures, throw pillows, or even small decor items. The warm and radiant tones of gold create a sense of opulence and refinement, making it a perfect choice for those seeking a touch of glamour in their living spaces. Uncover the secrets of gilded grandeur and transform your home into a haven of timeless elegance.

Silver Chic: A Modern Twist on Metallic Sophistication

Transition into "Silver Chic," where we explore the modern twist on metallic sophistication with the cool tones of silver. Silver accents bring a contemporary and sleek aesthetic to any decor style. From silver-framed mirrors to metallic wall sculptures, the reflective properties of silver add depth and dimension to your space.

Experiment with silver in combination with other materials like glass, acrylic, or mirrored surfaces for a chic and modern look. The versatility of silver allows it to seamlessly integrate with various color palettes, making it an ideal choice for those who appreciate a clean and sophisticated aesthetic. Dive into the world of silver chic and discover how this metallic hue can infuse your decor with a touch of modern glamour.

Bronze Beauty: Warming Up Your Space with Metallic Warmth

In the third section, "Bronze Beauty," we explore the rich and warm tones of bronze as a metallic accent in home decor. Bronze brings a sense of warmth and character to a space, making it an excellent choice for those who desire a more earthy and rustic feel. From bronze sculptures to accent furniture pieces, this versatile metallic finish adds a touch of antiquity and charm.

Consider pairing bronze with natural materials like wood or stone to enhance its warm and inviting qualities. Whether it's a bronze-toned chandelier or decorative accessories, the beauty of bronze lies in its ability to age gracefully, developing a unique patina over time. Embrace the timeless appeal of bronze beauty and bring a sense of warmth to your living space.

Mixed Metals: The Art of Harmonizing Metallic Finishes

Move on to "Mixed Metals," where we explore the art of harmonizing multiple metallic finishes within a single space. The days of adhering to a single metallic hue are long gone, and now, designers embrace the eclectic charm of mixing metals. Gold, silver, bronze, and even rose gold can coexist harmoniously, creating a visually dynamic and layered look.

Experiment with mixed-metal decor elements, such as a coffee table with gold and silver accents or a gallery wall featuring various metallic frames. The key to successfully incorporating mixed metals lies in maintaining a sense of balance and cohesion. Embrace the creative freedom that comes with mixing metals and discover how it can add depth and personality to your decor.

Artistic Illumination: Enhancing Lighting Fixtures with Metallic Finishes

Enter the fifth section, "Artistic Illumination," where we explore the transformative power of metallic finishes in lighting fixtures. Whether it's a stunning gold chandelier, a silver pendant light, or bronze sconces, the right lighting can elevate your decor to new heights. Metallic finishes in lighting not only serve a functional purpose but also act as sculptural pieces that enhance the overall aesthetic of a room.

Consider choosing a statement lighting fixture with metallic accents to become a focal point in your space. The play of light against the metallic surfaces adds a layer of drama and sophistication, creating a captivating ambiance. Dive into the world of artistic illumination and discover how metallic finishes in lighting can turn your home into a showcase of glamour and style.

DIY Metallic Magic: Crafting Personalized Accents with Metallic Paints

In the final section, "DIY Metallic Magic," we explore the creative and budget-friendly side of incorporating metallic accents through DIY projects. Metallic paints in gold, silver, and bronze open up a world of possibilities for transforming everyday items into personalized, glamorous accents. From furniture makeovers to decorative objects, unleash your creativity and infuse your home with a touch of handmade luxury.

Consider experimenting with stencils, geometric patterns, or ombre effects using metallic paints to add a custom touch to your decor. The satisfaction of creating your own metallic magic not only adds a personal flair to your space but also allows you to tailor the level of glamour to your taste. Embrace the DIY spirit and discover how metallic paints can turn ordinary items into extraordinary accents.

Conclusion:

As we conclude our journey through the world of golden elegance and metallic accents, remember that the key lies in finding the right balance for your personal style. Whether you're drawn to the timeless allure of gold, the modern chic of silver, the warm embrace of bronze, the eclectic charm of mixed metals, the artistic illumination of metallic lighting, or the DIY magic of metallic paints, each section has unveiled a facet of the glamorous possibilities metallic accents bring to your home.

WHIMSICAL WONDERS: EXPLORING THEMED WALL ART FOR KIDS' IMAGINATIVE SPACES

Step into the enchanting world of kids' rooms where creativity knows no bounds, and the walls become a canvas for endless possibilities. In this blog post, we'll embark on a playful journey, exploring the magic of themed wall art for children's spaces. From whimsical wonders to adventurous themes, join us in discovering how themed wall art can transform a room into a vibrant and imaginative haven for the little ones.

1. Beyond the Stars: Celestial Adventures in Kids' Wall Art:

Our first stop takes us beyond the stars, where celestial adventures unfold in the form of themed wall art for kids' rooms. Explore the cosmos with murals of planets, stars, and rocket ships that ignite the imagination. Consider glow-in-the-dark decals that mimic the night sky or framed prints featuring friendly aliens on intergalactic journeys.

Celestial-themed wall art creates a sense of wonder and curiosity, turning bedtime into an exciting cosmic exploration. From rocket-shaped shelves to constellation patterns, infuse the room with elements that evoke the magic of outer space. Beyond the stars, let your child's imagination soar to new heights as they drift off to dreamland surrounded by the enchanting allure of the universe.

2. Enchanted Forest: Bringing Nature's Whimsy Indoors with Woodland Wall Art:

Venture into the heart of an enchanted forest with woodland-themed wall art that brings nature's whimsy indoors. Imagine walls adorned with friendly animals, towering trees, and delicate butterflies. Opt for large murals that transport little ones to a magical woodland realm or choose framed prints that feature adorable forest creatures.

Woodland-themed wall art creates a soothing and imaginative atmosphere, fostering a connection with the wonders of nature. Consider incorporating 3D elements like tree branch hooks or animal-shaped wall shelves to enhance the immersive experience. Enchanted forest decor allows kids to explore the beauty of the outdoors right from the comfort of their own room, blending playfulness with the tranquility of nature.

3. Under the Sea: Dive into Oceanic Adventures with Marine Wall Art:

Dive into the depths of oceanic adventures with themed wall art that brings the wonders of the sea to life. Picture walls adorned with colorful fish, graceful dolphins, and majestic whales swimming through an underwater paradise. Opt for vibrant murals that span the entire room or mix and match framed prints to create a captivating marine gallery.

Under the sea-themed decor invites kids to explore the mysteries of the ocean, fostering a love for marine life and conservation. Consider incorporating elements like nautical-themed bedding, sea creature-shaped pillows, or even a hanging fishnet filled with stuffed animals. Dive deep into the imaginative world of under the sea-themed wall art, where every day feels like a journey beneath the waves.

4. Dinosaurs Roar: Prehistoric Playfulness in Dino-Inspired Wall Art:

Roar into the realm of prehistoric playfulness with dinosaur-themed wall art that turns kids' rooms into a Jurassic wonderland. Imagine walls adorned with towering dinosaurs, lush ferns, and volcanic landscapes. Opt for murals that transport young adventurers back in time or choose framed prints featuring their favorite dino species.

Dinosaur-themed decor sparks a sense of curiosity and excitement, making learning about prehistoric creatures an immersive experience. Consider adding 3D dinosaur decals that seem to leap from the walls or dinosaur-shaped rugs that create a playful and themed play area. Let the roars echo through the room as your little paleontologist explores the fascinating world of dinosaurs right at home.

5. Storybook Dreams: Literary Magic with Book-Inspired Wall Art:

Transform kids' rooms into realms of literary magic with book-inspired wall art that brings storybook dreams to life. Picture walls adorned with characters from beloved children's books, whimsical landscapes, and quotes that inspire imagination. Opt for murals that capture the essence of a favorite story or choose framed prints featuring characters from classic tales.

Book-inspired wall art fosters a love for reading and storytelling, creating an environment that celebrates the magic of literature. Consider incorporating a cozy reading nook with themed cushions, bookshelves filled with classic tales, or even a wall-mounted display for cherished storybooks. Let the pages of children's literature unfold on the walls, turning bedtime into a magical journey through the world of imagination.

6. Adventure Awaits: Travel-Themed Wall Art for Little Explorers:

Embark on a journey of adventure with travel-themed wall art that sparks the spirit of exploration in little ones. Picture walls adorned with maps, hot air balloons, and iconic landmarks from around the world. Opt for murals that transport kids to different continents or choose framed prints featuring modes of transportation and cultural elements.

Travel-themed decor encourages a sense of curiosity and a love for discovering new places. Consider incorporating interactive elements like a chalkboard map for marking visited destinations, a hanging globe for geographical exploration, or a DIY passport station for imaginative play. Adventure-themed wall art invites little

explorers to dream big and fosters a sense of wanderlust right within the comfort of their own space.

Conclusion:

As we conclude our journey through the whimsical wonders of themed wall art for kids' rooms, remember that these imaginative spaces serve as the backdrop for childhood dreams and adventures. Whether exploring the cosmos, diving into oceanic realms, or roaming with dinosaurs, themed wall art creates an environment where creativity knows no bounds. Let your child's room become a canvas for playful expression, where every wall tells a story, and every day is a new chapter in the book of childhood.

WANDER WALLS: ELEVATE YOUR HOME WITH TRAVEL-INSPIRED WALL ART

Embark on a journey within the walls of your home as we explore the enchanting world of travel-inspired wall art. In this blog post, we'll delve into the ways you can showcase your wanderlust and bring the spirit of your favorite destinations into your living space. From breathtaking landscapes to cultural vignettes, join us in discovering the art of transforming your home into a visual travelogue that reflects your passion for exploration.

1. Passport to Paradise: Creating a Travel Gallery Wall:

Our first destination on this visual journey is the creation of a passport to paradise – a travel gallery wall that encapsulates the essence of your wanderlust. Collect and curate a mix of travel souvenirs, postcards, and framed prints from your favorite destinations. Arrange them in an eclectic yet harmonious display that tells the story of your adventures around the globe.

Consider incorporating personal photographs taken during your travels, turning the gallery wall into a visual diary of your experiences. Experiment with different frame styles, sizes, and layouts to create a dynamic and eye-catching composition. The beauty of a travel gallery wall lies in its ability to transport you back to the places you've visited, evoking memories and igniting a sense of wanderlust every time you glance at the wall.

2. Cityscape Chronicles: Capturing Urban Vibes with Skylines and Landmarks:

Venture into the heart of urban landscapes as we explore the captivating world of cityscape chronicles. Capture the essence of your favorite cities with wall art featuring iconic skylines and landmarks. Whether it's the Eiffel Tower, the New York skyline, or the vibrant streets of Tokyo, cityscape wall art allows you to bring the energy and charm of urban life into your home.

Consider a large, statement piece that becomes the focal point of a room or create a curated collection of cityscapes that showcases the diversity of your travels. Cityscape wall art is not only visually stunning but also serves as a constant reminder of the cities that have left an indelible mark on your heart. Let the urban vibes flow through your home, turning walls into windows to the cities you love.

3. Wanderlust Watercolors: Infusing Soft Hues into Your Travel Aesthetic:

Dive into the gentle allure of wanderlust watercolors as we explore the softer side of travel-inspired wall art. Watercolor prints featuring landscapes, maps, or cultural scenes bring a delicate and artistic touch to your home. The soft hues and subtle brushstrokes create an atmosphere of tranquility, making wanderlust watercolors an ideal choice for bedrooms, reading nooks, or cozy corners.

Consider a series of watercolor prints that form a cohesive theme, such as a collection of landscapes from your favorite regions. The versatility of watercolor art allows it to seamlessly blend with various decor styles, from modern and minimalist to bohemian and eclectic. Infuse your space with the calming and dreamy aesthetic of wanderlust watercolors, turning walls into poetic canvases that echo the beauty of your travel memories.

4. Map Murals: Navigating Your Walls with Artistic Cartography:

Navigate your walls with the artistic allure of map murals, turning your space into a cartographic masterpiece. Map murals offer a unique and visually engaging way to showcase your wanderlust, allowing you to explore the world without leaving the comfort of your home. Choose a mural featuring the entire world or opt for a detailed map of a specific region that holds special significance to you.

Consider placing map murals in areas where they can serve as both decorative and educational elements. They make excellent additions to home offices, libraries, or even children's rooms, sparking a sense of curiosity and exploration. The intricate details of map murals, from coastlines to mountain ranges, add a layer of sophistication to your decor, making walls come alive with the spirit of adventure.

5. Cultural Collages: Celebrating Diversity with Artistic Montages:

Celebrate the diversity of the world's cultures with travel-inspired wall art in the form of cultural collages. Create artistic montages that showcase elements from various destinations, such as traditional patterns, architectural details, or cultural symbols. Cultural collages allow you to weave a tapestry of global influences that reflect your appreciation for the rich and varied traditions found across the globe.

Consider incorporating handmade crafts, textiles, or even elements like masks and sculptures into the collage for a tactile and multidimensional effect. The beauty of cultural collages lies in their ability to transport you to different corners of the world, fostering a sense of appreciation for the interconnectedness of humanity. Let your walls become a celebration of diversity, embracing the beauty of cultural exchange through artistic expression.

6. Personalized Travel Art: Turning Your Own Photos into Masterpieces:

Conclude our journey by exploring the world of personalized travel art, where your own photographs take center stage as masterpieces on your walls. Turn your most cherished travel photos into canvas prints, framed artworks, or even create a photo wall that spans an entire room. Personalized travel art adds an intimate touch to your home, allowing you to relive the moments that have shaped your wanderlust.

Consider selecting a theme for your personalized travel art, such as a collection of beach sunsets, mountain adventures, or snapshots of local markets. The ability to turn your own photos into art ensures that your space is not only visually appealing but also deeply personal. Transform your walls into a gallery of your own adventures, and let the stories behind each photograph become an integral part of your home's decor.

Conclusion:

As we conclude our journey through the world of travel-inspired wall art, remember that your home is not just a place to live but a canvas to express your passions and experiences. Whether you choose to create a gallery wall, showcase cityscapes, embrace wanderlust watercolors, navigate with map murals, celebrate diversity with cultural collages, or personalize your space with travel photos, let your walls become a testament to the incredible journey of a life well-traveled.

ELEGANCE UNVEILED: THE ALLURE OF MONOCHROMATIC MAGIC IN BLACK AND WHITE ART

Dive into a world of timeless sophistication as we explore the enchanting allure of monochromatic magic in black and white art. In this blog post, we'll uncover the design potential of this classic color scheme, discovering how the simplicity of black and white transforms your living space into a canvas of elegance. From minimalist masterpieces to bold statements, join us on a journey through the captivating realm of black and white art that transcends trends and stands the test of time.

1. The Art of Contrast: Creating Drama and Impact with Black and White Art:

Our first destination on this monochromatic journey is the art of contrast, where black and white unite to create dramatic and impactful compositions. Black and white art thrives on the dynamic interplay between light and dark, drawing the eye with a striking visual contrast. This powerful combination allows for bold statements and eye-catching focal points, making it an ideal choice for those looking to infuse their space with a touch of drama.

Consider choosing artworks that utilize strong contrasts, such as black and white photography with bold shadows or abstract pieces with sharp lines and shapes. The art of contrast extends beyond traditional paintings to include sculptures, textiles, and even furniture. Let your space come alive with the energy of black and white contrast, turning walls into dynamic canvases that command attention.

2. Minimalist Marvels: Embracing Simplicity with Black and White Minimalism:

Venture into the realm of minimalist marvels, where black and white art embraces simplicity to create a clean and refined aesthetic. Minimalism in black and white allows for a serene and uncluttered atmosphere, making it an excellent choice for those who appreciate a modern and understated design. The absence of color highlights form and composition, allowing each element to speak for itself.

Consider incorporating black and white minimalist art in spaces where clarity and tranquility are desired, such as bedrooms, home offices, or living rooms. Minimalist marvels go beyond wall art to include furnishings, decor, and even architectural elements. Embrace the simplicity of black and white minimalism, and let your space become a haven of calm sophistication.

3. Timeless Classics: The Enduring Appeal of Black and White Photography:

Step into the world of timeless classics with black and white photography, where the absence of color enhances the emotional impact of each captured moment. Black and white photography transcends trends, offering a sense of nostalgia and timelessness that resonates across generations. From iconic portraits to breathtaking landscapes, black and white photography adds a touch of artistry to your space.

Consider curating a gallery wall of black and white photographs that tell a visual story or selecting a single, powerful image as a focal point. The versatility of black and white photography makes it suitable for various design styles, from vintage and rustic to modern and industrial. Embrace the enduring appeal of timeless classics, and let your walls become a gallery of captured memories and evocative moments.

4. Abstract Elegance: Exploring Form and Expression in Black and White Abstract Art:

Embark on a journey into abstract elegance, where black and white abstract art takes center stage in exploring form, expression, and the interplay of shapes. Abstract black and white art opens the door to interpretation, allowing viewers to engage with the artwork on a personal and emotional level. The absence of color invites attention to composition, movement, and the subtle nuances of light and shadow.

Consider selecting abstract pieces that resonate with your individual style and preferences, whether it's bold and energetic strokes or delicate and intricate patterns. Abstract elegance extends beyond traditional canvases to include sculptures, textiles, and even murals. Embrace the freedom of expression in black and white abstract art, and let your walls become a canvas for the exploration of form and emotion.

5. Black and White in Interior Design: Infusing Modern Spaces with Timeless Chic:

Discover the transformative power of black and white in interior design, where these classic hues infuse modern spaces with timeless chic. Black and white art becomes an integral part of a cohesive design scheme, allowing for versatility and adaptability. The neutral palette provides a clean backdrop for other design elements, making it easy to incorporate a variety of textures, materials, and accent colors.

Consider using black and white art as a focal point in rooms with neutral color schemes, allowing the artwork to shine as a central element. The integration of black and white in interior design extends to furniture, textiles, and decor accessories. Embrace the timeless chic of this classic color combination, and watch as your living space becomes a testament to the enduring elegance of black and white.

6. Personal Expression: Customizing Your Space with Black and White Artwork:

Conclude our exploration by delving into personal expression, where black and white art becomes a canvas for customizing your space with a touch of individuality. Many artists offer bespoke black and white artworks, allowing you to collaborate on pieces that resonate with your personality and preferences. Customizing your space with black and white artwork ensures that your walls tell a unique story that reflects your style.

Consider working with an artist to create a piece that incorporates meaningful symbols, personal mementos, or even a representation of your favorite places. Personal expression through black and white art goes beyond traditional paintings to include murals, installations, and mixed-media creations. Let your walls become a reflection of your unique identity, infusing your living space with the warmth and authenticity of personal expression.

Conclusion:

As we conclude our journey through the world of monochromatic magic in black and white art, remember that the beauty of this classic color scheme lies in its versatility, timelessness, and ability to evoke a range of emotions. Whether you're drawn to the drama of contrast, the simplicity of minimalism, the enduring appeal of timeless classics, the exploration of abstract elegance, the chic integration in interior design, or the personal expression of customized artwork, let your walls become a canvas of elegance and sophistication. Elevate your living space with the allure of black and white art and watch as your walls transform into a timeless masterpiece.

HARMONY UNVEILED: MASTERING FENG SHUI WITH WALL ART FOR POSITIVE ENERGY FLOW

Step into a world where ancient wisdom meets contemporary aesthetics as we explore the union of Feng Shui and wall art. In this blog post, "Harmony Unveiled," we'll delve into the transformative power of art in enhancing the energy flow within your home. From creating serene havens of tranquility to fostering spaces of vitality and creativity, join us on a journey through the art of Feng Shui and discover how your walls can become conduits of positive energy.

The Art of Placement: Arranging Wall Art for Chi Circulation

Embark on our journey with "The Art of Placement," where we unravel the essence of Feng Shui in arranging wall art for optimal chi circulation. Consider the Bagua map, a Feng Shui tool that divides your space into nine areas, each representing a different aspect of life. Explore how specific wall art placements within these areas can influence the flow of energy and enhance corresponding aspects of your life.

Whether it's placing serene landscapes in the Health and Family area or vibrant abstracts in the Creativity and Fame zone, the art of placement goes beyond mere aesthetics. It becomes a deliberate act of channeling positive energy throughout your home. Uncover the secrets of arranging your wall art to invite harmony and balance into every corner.

Elemental Balance: Infusing Five Elements into Your Wall Art

Transition into "Elemental Balance," where we explore the infusion of the five elements—Wood, Fire, Earth, Metal, and Water—into your wall art. In Feng Shui, each element corresponds to specific aspects of life and carries its own energy. Discover how selecting art that represents or complements these elements creates a harmonious balance, fostering a dynamic flow of energy within your space.

Consider incorporating wooden frames for the Wood element, fiery red hues for Fire, or metallic finishes for Metal. The elemental balance in your wall art not only adds visual interest but also aligns with the principles of Feng Shui, promoting a sense of equilibrium and vitality. Immerse yourself in the art of elemental infusion and witness the transformative energy it brings.

Color Magic: Harnessing Feng Shui Colors for Positive Vibes

In the third section, "Color Magic," we explore the profound impact of Feng Shui colors in wall art on the energy of your living space. Each color carries its own energy and symbolism, influencing the atmosphere and emotions within a room. Dive into the world of color psychology within Feng Shui, from calming blues and greens to energizing reds and yellows.

Consider selecting wall art that aligns with the desired energy for a particular room. A tranquil bedroom may benefit from serene blues, while a lively living room could thrive with the vibrancy of reds and oranges. Discover how harnessing Feng Shui colors in your wall art choices creates a visually appealing and energetically charged environment that resonates with positivity.

Reflective Wisdom: Mirrors and Art for Expanding Space and Energy

Move on to "Reflective Wisdom," where we explore the strategic use of mirrors in conjunction with wall art to expand both physical space and energy. Mirrors in Feng Shui are known for their ability to amplify energy and reflect light, creating a sense of openness and abundance. When strategically combined with art, mirrors become powerful tools for enhancing the flow of positive chi.

Consider placing mirrors adjacent to wall art to visually expand the space and reflect the beauty of your chosen pieces. This combination not only brings depth to your decor but also magnifies the energetic impact of your art. Delve into the reflective wisdom of Feng Shui and discover how mirrors and art together can transform confined spaces into expansive havens.

Nature's Bounty: Integrating Natural Elements Through Wall Art

Enter the fifth section, "Nature's Bounty," where we explore the integration of natural elements in wall art to connect with the Earth's energy. Feng Shui emphasizes the importance of grounding and connecting with nature to enhance well-being. Discover how incorporating art featuring landscapes, flora, or fauna brings the rejuvenating essence of the outdoors into your indoor spaces.

Consider selecting wall art that resonates with your personal connection to nature, whether it's a serene beach scene, a lush forest, or botanical prints. This infusion of natural elements not only beautifies your walls but also infuses your home with the grounding energy of the Earth. Immerse yourself in the bounty of nature's embrace through carefully curated wall art.

Personalized Energy: Infusing Your Intentions into Custom Wall Art

In the final section, "Personalized Energy," we explore the transformative power of infusing your intentions and personal energy into custom wall art. Feng Shui encourages the intentional selection of art that resonates with your goals, aspirations, and the energy you wish to manifest in your life.

Consider collaborating with artists to create custom pieces that reflect your personal journey, values, or aspirations. Whether it's a vision board-style collage or a commissioned piece inspired by your intentions, personalized wall art becomes a tangible expression of your desires. Unleash the power of your personal energy into your living space through custom creations that align with the principles of Feng Shui.

Conclusion:

As we conclude our journey through the symbiotic relationship between Feng Shui and wall art, remember that each piece you choose has the potential to be more than just a decoration. It can be a conduit for positive energy, a source of inspiration, and a reflection of your intentions. Whether you're arranging art for chi circulation, infusing elemental balance, harnessing color magic, employing reflective wisdom, embracing nature's bounty, or personalizing your energy, the art of Feng Shui is an ongoing journey toward creating a harmonious and energized living space.

BLANK CANVAS BRILLIANCE: THE MAGIC OF WHITEWASHED WALLS AND BRIGHT ART

Step into a realm of freshness and vibrancy as we explore the enchanting combination of whitewashed walls and bright art. In this blog post, "Blank Canvas Brilliance," we'll uncover the secrets of creating a light and airy atmosphere with the blank canvas of whitewashed walls, allowing your vibrant art to take center stage. From the allure of a minimalist backdrop to the dynamic energy of bold hues, discover how this pairing transforms your space into a haven of brightness and creativity.

The Allure of Whitewashed Walls: A Minimalist Canvas for Possibilities

Embark on our journey with "The Allure of Whitewashed Walls," where we delve into the minimalist charm of this timeless backdrop. Whitewashed walls offer a neutral and clean canvas that serves as the perfect foundation for any design style. The subtle elegance of white tones creates a sense of openness and purity, making your space feel larger and more inviting.

Consider the versatility of whitewashed walls as a backdrop for various decor styles, from Scandinavian simplicity to coastal chic. The minimalist allure of whitewashed walls is the ideal starting point for those seeking a fresh and timeless aesthetic. Uncover the magic of a blank canvas that invites endless possibilities and sets the stage for the brilliance of bright art.

Bright Art Energizes: Infusing Life into Whitewashed Spaces

Transition into "Bright Art Energizes," where we explore how vibrant and colorful art infuses life into the serene canvas of whitewashed walls. Whether it's a bold abstract painting, a collection of lively prints, or eclectic wall sculptures, the introduction of bright art creates a dynamic contrast against the neutral backdrop. The interplay of white and bright hues brings a burst of energy and personality to your living space.

Experiment with a mix of colors, from vibrant primaries to soothing pastels, depending on the mood you want to evoke. Bright art not only serves as a visual focal point but also reflects your personality and style. Dive into the world of energizing contrasts and discover how the infusion of lively art transforms your whitewashed walls into a gallery of brilliance.

Gallery Wall Galore: Crafting Visual Stories on Whitewashed Canvases

In the third section, "Gallery Wall Galore," we explore the art of crafting visual stories on whitewashed canvases through curated gallery walls. Whitewashed walls provide the perfect backdrop for creating personalized and captivating displays. Whether it's a collection of family photos, a gallery of travel memories, or an eclectic mix of artistic expressions, gallery walls add depth and interest to your space.

Experiment with different frame styles, sizes, and arrangements to achieve a harmonious yet eclectic look. The beauty of gallery walls lies in their ability to tell a visual story that evolves over time. Embrace the creative freedom of arranging art on your whitewashed walls and transform them into a dynamic canvas that narrates your unique story.

Bold Hues on Neutral Ground: Making a Statement with Bright Furniture

Move on to "Bold Hues on Neutral Ground," where we explore the impact of incorporating bright furniture against the neutral canvas of whitewashed walls. While art takes center stage, strategically placing furniture in vibrant hues amplifies the overall impact. Whether it's a bold sofa, colorful chairs, or vibrant accent pieces, the introduction of bright furniture creates a cohesive and visually striking design.

Consider selecting furniture in complementary or contrasting colors to achieve the desired effect. The juxtaposition of neutral walls and vivid furniture not only adds a touch of playfulness but also establishes a balanced and well-coordinated look. Immerse yourself in the world of bold hues on neutral ground and discover how bright furniture makes a stylish statement against whitewashed walls.

Natural Elements: Bringing the Outdoors In with Bright Botanicals

Enter the fifth section, "Natural Elements," where we explore the refreshing combination of whitewashed walls and bright botanical art. Nature-inspired art featuring vibrant florals, lush greenery, or tropical motifs brings the outdoors in, creating a sense of freshness and tranquility. Whitewashed walls serve as the perfect backdrop, allowing the colors and textures of botanical art to shine.

Consider selecting art that reflects your favorite elements of nature, whether it's a vibrant floral print or a lush landscape. The synergy between whitewashed walls and bright botanicals creates a serene and harmonious atmosphere, evoking the beauty of nature within your living space. Immerse yourself in the soothing embrace of natural elements against a neutral canvas.

DIY Bright Art Projects: Adding a Personal Touch to Whitewashed Walls

In the final section, "DIY Bright Art Projects," we explore the joy of adding a personal touch to whitewashed walls through vibrant and creative DIY projects. Unleash your inner artist and embark on a journey of self-expression, whether it's painting your own abstract canvas, creating a collage of colorful prints, or experimenting with unique art techniques.

Consider involving the entire family in DIY art projects to infuse a sense of unity and personal connection to your living space. The beauty of DIY bright art is not only in the finished creation but also in the process of self-discovery and creativity. Embrace the joy of crafting personalized art that adorns your whitewashed walls with unique stories and memories.

Conclusion:

As we conclude our journey through the magic of whitewashed walls and bright art, remember that the key lies in finding the perfect balance that resonates with your style and personality. Whether you're drawn to the allure of minimalist canvases, the energizing impact of bright art, the storytelling charm of gallery walls, the statement-making bold hues, the refreshing embrace of natural elements, or the joy of DIY projects, each section unveils a facet of the brilliance that emerges when whitewashed walls meet bright art.

ARTISTIC LIGHTING: ILLUMINATING YOUR PROPERTY'S VALUE

Shedding Light on the Art of Illumination

"Artistic Lighting: Illuminating Your Property's Value" unveils the transformative power of lighting as a strategic element in enhancing your property's aesthetic appeal and overall value. Join us on a radiant journey through creative lighting solutions that go beyond functionality to create an artful ambiance.

"The Luminous Landscape: Crafting Ambiance with Outdoor Lighting"

In "The Luminous Landscape," explore the world of outdoor lighting and its profound impact on your property's curb appeal. From pathway lanterns to tree uplighting, discover how carefully designed outdoor lighting can turn your garden into a mesmerizing nighttime oasis, adding both beauty and value to your property.

"Statement Fixtures: Lighting as Sculptural Art"

Delve into the concept of "Statement Fixtures," where lighting becomes more than just a practical necessity. Uncover how sculptural light fixtures can serve as focal points, transforming living spaces into curated galleries. From elegant chandeliers to avant-garde pendant lights, learn how lighting choices can redefine the artistic character of your home.

"Dynamic Color Play: Illuminating Your Mood with Smart Lighting"

Explore the interactive world of "Dynamic Color Play," where smart lighting takes center stage. Understand how programmable LED lights can be used to create versatile atmospheres, adapting to different occasions and moods. Dive into the possibilities of transforming your living spaces with a simple touch, adding an artistic and dynamic dimension to your property.

"Architectural Accents: Illuminating Unique Property Features"

In "Architectural Accents," discover how lighting can be used to highlight and accentuate the unique features of your property. Whether it's illuminating intricate architectural details, showcasing textured walls, or emphasizing specific design elements, strategic lighting can draw attention to the property's distinctive character, enhancing its overall value.

"Artful Task Lighting: Combining Functionality with Aesthetics"

Uncover the harmony between functionality and aesthetics in "Artful Task Lighting." Explore how task lighting, typically associated with practicality, can be transformed into an artistic expression. From kitchen islands to study nooks, understand how carefully selected task lighting can enhance both functionality and visual appeal.

"Eco-Friendly Illumination: Sustainable Lighting for Modern Homes"

Conclude our exploration with "Eco-Friendly Illumination," where we shed light on sustainable lighting choices. Learn how energy-efficient fixtures, LED technologies, and solar-powered options not only contribute to a greener environment but also elevate the eco-friendly profile of your property, adding a unique dimension to its overall value.

ART CONSULTATION SERVICES: ELEVATING OUR SPACE WITH PROFESSIONAL EXPERTISE

The Art of Transformation - Unlocking the Potential of Your Space

Embark on a transformative journey as we explore the invaluable role of "Art Consultation Services" in enhancing the aesthetic appeal and market value of your property. Discover how professional advice can turn your space into a curated masterpiece, reflecting your personality and captivating potential buyers.

"Navigating the Artistic Landscape: The Need for Guidance"

In "Navigating the Artistic Landscape," we delve into the complexities of the art world and why seeking professional advice is crucial. Explore the myriad options available and how an art consultant can help you navigate the vast landscape, ensuring that every piece chosen aligns seamlessly with your vision and the property's character.

"Tailored Aesthetics: Customizing Art to Your Space"

Explore "Tailored Aesthetics" and understand how art consultation services go beyond generic recommendations. Dive into the process of customizing artworks to fit your space perfectly, considering factors like size, color schemes, and thematic elements that harmonize with your property's unique features.

"Budgeting Brilliance: Maximizing Impact Within Constraints"

In "Budgeting Brilliance," discover the art of maximizing impact within budget constraints. Uncover how art consultants excel in curating a collection that aligns with your financial parameters while ensuring each piece contributes significantly to the overall ambiance and aesthetic appeal.

"Strategic Placement: The Art of Spatial Harmony"

Explore "Strategic Placement" and learn how art consultants excel in the delicate art of spatial harmony. Delve into the significance of placing artworks thoughtfully, creating focal points that draw attention to your property's best features while enhancing the overall flow and ambiance.

Section 5: "Curation with Purpose: Enhancing the Property's Story"

In "Curation with Purpose," understand how art consultation services add a layer of narrative to your property. Discover the strategic curation that weaves a story, making your space more engaging and emotionally resonant for potential buyers, transforming it into a place they can envision calling home.

"The Investment Perspective: Art as a Property Asset"

Conclude our journey with "The Investment Perspective," exploring how art consultation services can enhance your property's overall value. Understand the long-term benefits of strategic art investments and how they contribute to the property's market appeal, making it a more attractive prospect for potential buyers.

THEATRICAL DRAMA: BOLD ART CHOICES FOR STATEMENT INTERIORS

Step into the limelight of interior design with "Theatrical Drama: Bold Art Choices for Statement Interiors." In this blog post, we will explore the exhilarating world of bold art, guiding you through the impactful decisions that can transform your living spaces into captivating stages. Unleash your creativity and make a statement with every brushstroke, color choice, and artistic expression.

Embracing the Spotlight: The Power of Oversized Art

In "Embracing the Spotlight," we dive headfirst into the dramatic allure of oversized art. Discover how a single, bold statement piece can redefine the entire ambiance of a room. Whether it's a massive canvas, an imposing sculpture, or a mural that spans an entire wall, learn how to command attention and set the stage for theatrical drama.

Consider selecting a piece that resonates with your personality, pushing the boundaries of conventional size for an unforgettable visual impact. Embracing the Spotlight is about making a bold entrance into the world of statement interiors.

Color Explosion: Vibrant Hues and Vivid Tones

In "Color Explosion," we explore the transformative power of vibrant hues and vivid tones. Dive into the world of bold, saturated colors that can evoke emotions and create a dynamic atmosphere. From fiery reds to electric blues, learn how to infuse your space with energy and excitement through your art choices.

Consider opting for artwork that features a bold color palette or a mix of contrasting shades to add a touch of drama. Color Explosion invites you to embrace the full spectrum of possibilities and turn your living space into a vibrant canvas.

Eclectic Elegance: Mixing Styles for Artistic Diversity

In "Eclectic Elegance," we celebrate the art of mixing styles to create a visually rich and dynamic environment. Discover how juxtaposing different art forms, from classic paintings to modern sculptures, can add layers of sophistication and drama to your interiors. Learn the art of curating an eclectic collection that tells a story.

Consider combining unexpected elements, such as a vintage painting alongside a contemporary sculpture, to create a harmonious yet eclectic narrative. Eclectic Elegance encourages you to break free from the conventional and embrace the beauty of artistic diversity.

Gallery Wall Grandeur: Curating a Narrative

In "Gallery Wall Grandeur," we shift our focus to the captivating world of curated collections. Explore how a well-thought-out gallery wall can turn your space into a visual masterpiece. From arranging artwork in a cohesive theme to creating a narrative that unfolds across your walls, learn the secrets of gallery wall curation.

Consider selecting pieces that share a common theme, whether it's a specific color palette, subject matter, or artistic style. Gallery Wall Grandeur is about transforming your home into a personal art gallery that leaves a lasting impression.

Textured Tales: Adding Depth with Sculptural Art

In "Textured Tales," we explore the role of sculptural art in adding depth and dimension to your interiors. Discover how three-dimensional pieces can create a multisensory experience, inviting touch and exploration. From abstract sculptures to intricate installations, learn how to make a powerful statement with art that transcends the two-dimensional.

Consider incorporating textured artwork made from materials like metal, wood, or ceramics to add a tactile element to your space. Textured Tales invites you to sculpt a narrative that goes beyond the visual and engages the senses.

Lighting as Art: Illuminating the Dramatic

In "Lighting as Art," we conclude our theatrical journey by shedding light on the transformative power of artistic lighting. Explore how unconventional light fixtures and installations can become integral elements of your bold interior design. From sculptural chandeliers to avant-garde floor lamps, discover the artistry in illuminating your space.

Consider choosing lighting fixtures that not only serve a functional purpose but also act as striking art pieces on their own. Lighting as Art encourages you to play with shadows, create focal points, and elevate your interiors through the magic of light.

Conclusion:

As the curtains fall on "Theatrical Drama: Bold Art Choices for Statement Interiors," let your home become the stage for your personal artistic expression. From oversized statements to vibrant explosions of color, embrace the drama and make a lasting impression with every design decision. Redefine your living spaces and let them become a canvas for the extraordinary.

SYMMETRICAL SERENITY: CREATING CALMNESS WITH BALANCED ART

Step into the world of tranquility and visual harmony with "Symmetrical Serenity: Creating Calmness with Balanced Art." In this blog post, we embark on a journey to explore the calming effects of symmetrical art arrangements, guiding you on how to achieve a sense of equilibrium in your living spaces.

The Art of Symmetry: A Visual Foundation

In "The Art of Symmetry," we delve into the fundamentals of creating a visual foundation based on balance and proportion. Discover how symmetrical arrangements can provide a sense of stability and order, setting the stage for a serene atmosphere. From perfectly aligned frames to mirrored compositions, learn the art of using symmetry as a powerful design tool.

Consider incorporating symmetrical elements in furniture, decor, and art to establish a cohesive and visually pleasing foundation. The Art of Symmetry is your gateway to understanding the core principles of balanced aesthetics.

Mirrored Magic: Doubling the Serenity

In "Mirrored Magic," we explore the enchanting effects of mirrored symmetry. Uncover the transformative power of using identical art pieces or reflections to create a sense of spaciousness and tranquility. Learn how mirrored arrangements can amplify natural light, making your space feel brighter and more open.

Consider choosing identical pieces of art or strategically placing mirrors to achieve a mirrored effect on your walls. Mirrored Magic invites you to double the serenity and enhance the peaceful ambiance of your living areas.

Symmetry in Nature: Bringing the Outdoors In

In "Symmetry in Nature," we draw inspiration from the natural world, exploring how symmetrical patterns in art can evoke a connection to the outdoors. Discover the calming influence of nature-inspired symmetrical designs, from floral motifs to geometric patterns reminiscent of natural formations.

Consider incorporating art that mirrors the symmetry found in the natural world, bringing a touch of the outdoors into your interior spaces. Symmetry in Nature is about harmonizing your living environment with the calming patterns of the Earth.

Furniture Symmetry: Balancing Art and Decor

In "Furniture Symmetry," we shift our focus to the interplay between symmetrical art arrangements and furniture placement. Explore how the positioning of furniture can complement and enhance the calming effects of balanced art. Learn the art of creating cohesive living spaces that promote relaxation and comfort.

Consider arranging furniture in symmetrical patterns around your art to create a seamless and unified visual experience. Furniture Symmetry guides you in achieving a holistic design approach that extends beyond the walls.

Symmetry in Color: Creating Calm Color Palettes

In "Symmetry in Color," we examine the role of color harmony in enhancing the serenity of symmetrical art displays. Discover how a balanced color palette can contribute to a calm and soothing atmosphere. From monochromatic schemes to carefully coordinated hues, learn the art of using color symmetry to evoke a sense of tranquility.

Consider selecting art pieces with colors that complement each other, creating a unified and peaceful visual experience. Symmetry in Color invites you to explore the calming influence of harmonious color arrangements.

Flowing Symmetry: Guiding the Eye

In "Flowing Symmetry," we conclude our exploration by understanding how symmetrical arrangements can guide the eye through a space. Explore the concept of flowing symmetry, where the viewer's gaze effortlessly moves from one balanced element to another, creating a continuous and calming visual flow.

Consider arranging art pieces in a way that directs the viewer's attention with a sense of ease and rhythm. Flowing Symmetry encourages you to create a harmonious journey for the eyes, enhancing the overall serenity of your living spaces.

Conclusion:

As we wrap up our journey through "Symmetrical Serenity," let the principles of balanced art arrangements guide you in creating calm and peaceful interiors. Embrace symmetry as a powerful tool to achieve visual harmony and transform your living spaces into havens of tranquility.

SCANDINAVIAN SIMPLICITY: MINIMALIST ART FOR MODERN SPACES

Welcome to the serene realm of Scandinavian Simplicity, where less is indeed more. In this blog post, we'll explore the captivating world of minimalist art and its seamless integration into modern spaces. Embrace the beauty of simplicity as we guide you through the nuances of Scandinavian design principles and the art that complements it.

Embracing Hygge: Cozy Minimalism for Every Room

In "Embracing Hygge," we delve into the heart of Scandinavian coziness and how minimalist art plays a pivotal role in achieving that warm, inviting atmosphere. Discover how neutral color palettes, natural materials, and carefully selected minimalist art pieces can transform your living spaces into havens of tranquility.

Consider incorporating soft, abstract prints or monochromatic line art that evoke a sense of calm and balance. Embrace Hygge and let your home become a sanctuary of comfort and style.

Nordic Nature: Bringing the Outdoors In with Minimalist Art

In "Nordic Nature," we explore the deep connection between Scandinavian design and nature. Discover how minimalist art can capture the essence of Nordic landscapes, bringing the beauty of the outdoors into your living room. From serene forest prints to abstract representations of the changing seasons, learn how to infuse your space with a touch of natural elegance.

Consider incorporating botanical line drawings or subtle landscape prints that reflect the simplicity and beauty of the Nordic environment. Nordic Nature invites you to create a harmonious blend of indoors and outdoors within your home.

Monochrome Magic: The Power of Black and White in Minimalist Art

In "Monochrome Magic," we unravel the timeless allure of black and white in Scandinavian design. Explore the versatility of monochromatic art, from bold contrasts to subtle gradients, and learn how to use this classic palette to create striking focal points. Dive into the world of minimalism where every line and shade tells a story.

Consider adorning your walls with black and white photography or abstract line art that makes a powerful statement. Monochrome Magic celebrates the simplicity of grayscale, letting your art speak volumes without uttering a single word.

Functional Aesthetics: The Marriage of Form and Function

In "Functional Aesthetics," we explore the Scandinavian philosophy of merging form and function. Learn how minimalist art can be both visually appealing and purposeful, seamlessly integrating into your daily life. From wall-mounted shelves with integrated art displays to multifunctional furniture with built-in artwork, discover ways to make your living space aesthetically pleasing and practical.

Consider selecting art pieces that serve a dual purpose, such as a wall clock with an artistic design or a decorative mirror with minimalist flair. Functional Aesthetics encourages you to embrace the practical side of minimalist art.

Whimsical Geometry: Playful Patterns in Minimalist Art

In "Whimsical Geometry," we celebrate the playful side of Scandinavian design, exploring how geometric patterns and shapes can add a touch of whimsy to your minimalist art collection. Discover the beauty of simplicity in geometric prints and how these elements can infuse your space with a sense of order and charm.

Consider incorporating minimalist prints featuring triangles, circles, or hexagons to add a dash of geometry to your walls. Whimsical Geometry encourages you to have fun with patterns while staying true to the clean lines of minimalist design.

The Art of Negative Space: Creating Balance and Harmony

In "The Art of Negative Space," we unravel the importance of leaving room for simplicity. Explore how the deliberate use of empty spaces in minimalist art contributes to a sense of balance and harmony in your interiors. Learn the art of curating a collection where each piece complements the others, allowing your space to breathe.

Consider selecting artwork with substantial negative space, allowing the simplicity of the design to shine through. The Art of Negative Space encourages you to appreciate the beauty of less and to let each piece hold its own within the overall composition.

Conclusion:

As we conclude our journey into the world of "Scandinavian Simplicity: Minimalist Art for Modern Spaces," let your home be a canvas of tranquility. From Embracing Hygge to The Art of Negative Space, each section celebrates the elegance of simplicity and its profound impact on modern living. Transform your space into a haven of minimalist art and experience the beauty of Scandinavian design.

ARTISTRY UNLEASHED: A COMPREHENSIVE GUIDE TO CUSTOMIZING ART SPACES IN YOUR HOME DECOR

The Canvas of Your Home - Art as the Heart of Decor

Incorporating art into your home decor is not just about hanging a few paintings; it's about creating a curated space that reflects your personality and style. In this guide, we'll explore the art of customizing your living spaces with creativity, from choosing the right pieces to arranging them thoughtfully.

Gallery Wall Galore - Crafting a Personalized Art Showcase

The gallery wall is a timeless trend that transforms any space into an art lover's haven. Start by choosing a focal point—a wall in the living room, above the staircase, or even a dedicated hallway. Mix and match various-sized frames and artwork styles, ensuring a harmonious blend of colors and themes. Transitioning from the conventional grid layout, experiment with asymmetry for a more eclectic and dynamic display.

Consider incorporating a mix of personal photos, travel souvenirs, and DIY art for a truly unique gallery. The gallery wall is a visual storytelling opportunity; let it narrate your journey and interests. As you arrange the pieces, pay attention to spacing and balance to create a cohesive yet captivating composition. This personalized gallery becomes a visual feast and a conversation starter for anyone who enters your home.

Artful Accents - Infusing Small Spaces with Big Statements

If you have limited wall space, don't underestimate the power of artful accents to make a big impact. From statement vases and sculptures to decorative throw pillows and blankets, infuse your home with artistic elements that complement your overall aesthetic. Consider investing in unique, handcrafted pieces that add character to your space.

Experiment with DIY projects, such as creating a personalized art installation with floating shelves or showcasing small artworks on a decorative ladder. The key is to think beyond traditional wall hangings and find unconventional ways to incorporate art into every nook and cranny. These artful accents not only enhance your decor but also bring a sense of creativity and personality to even the smallest corners of your home.

Functional Art - Elevating Everyday Items

Transforming everyday items into pieces of art is a delightful way to customize your living spaces. Look for functional items with artistic flair, such as a hand-painted teapot, artist-designed dinnerware, or a sculptural lamp. Choose pieces that seamlessly blend form and function, enhancing the visual appeal of your home while serving practical purposes.

Consider incorporating custom-made furniture or reimagining existing pieces with artistic touches. A painted accent wall, a handcrafted coffee table, or even creatively framed mirrors can become functional art pieces. This approach not only adds visual interest to your home but also transforms the ordinary into the extraordinary, making every aspect of your living space a canvas for artistic expression.

Colorful Conversations - Using Art to Define Color Palettes

Art has the magical ability to inspire color palettes that can define the entire ambiance of your home. Use your favorite artwork as a starting point for choosing wall colors, furniture, and decor accents. Pick out key colors from your artwork and incorporate them strategically throughout the room to create a cohesive and harmonious look.

Experiment with contrasting and complementary colors to add depth and visual interest. Consider the emotional impact of different colors; warm tones like reds and oranges can create a cozy atmosphere, while cool blues and greens evoke a sense of calm. Let the colors within your artwork guide your choices, turning your home into a vibrant and visually pleasing masterpiece.

Rotating Art Exhibits - Keeping Things Fresh and Inspiring

Just as art galleries rotate exhibits to keep things fresh, consider adopting the same approach in your home. Periodically switch out artwork to reflect the changing seasons, your evolving tastes, or simply to keep the decor dynamic. Create a designated space for a rotating art display—a feature wall, a dedicated art nook, or even a revolving display system.

This approach not only allows you to showcase a variety of pieces but also prevents your decor from becoming stagnant. Consider borrowing artworks from friends or exploring local artist collaborations to introduce new perspectives into your home. The rotating art exhibit keeps your living spaces inspiring, ever-changing, and a true reflection of your current artistic inclinations.

DIY Art Projects - Personalized Creations for a Truly Unique Home

Embrace your inner artist by incorporating do-it-yourself (DIY) art projects into your home decor. Create personalized canvases, abstract paintings, or even customized wall hangings that align with your aesthetic vision. Experiment with different materials, textures, and styles to craft pieces that are not only visually appealing but also hold sentimental value.

Involve your family in DIY art projects, turning them into collaborative endeavors that add an extra layer of warmth and personal connection to your home. From hand-painted furniture to homemade tapestries, the possibilities are endless. DIY art projects not only make your home uniquely yours but also provide a therapeutic and fulfilling outlet for your creative expression.

Conclusion: Artistry Unleashed - Your Home as a Living Canvas

In conclusion, customizing your living spaces with art is a celebration of personal expression and creativity. Whether it's through gallery walls, functional art, or DIY projects, let your home be a living canvas that evolves with your artistic journey. Infuse every corner with pieces that inspire, comfort, and tell the story of who you are. Your home is not just a place; it's a masterpiece in the making.

BRUSHING AWAY STRESS: YOUR ULTIMATE GUIDE TO DIY ART PROJECTS FOR RELAXATION

The Therapeutic Touch of Art

In the hustle and bustle of daily life, finding moments of calm is essential for mental well-being. Engaging in do-it-yourself (DIY) art projects provides a creative escape, offering a therapeutic outlet to alleviate stress and promote relaxation. In this comprehensive guide, we'll explore various DIY art projects that are not only enjoyable but also effective in helping you unwind and recharge.

1: Paint Your Serenity - The Healing Power of Canvas

Dive into the world of painting as a form of stress relief. Set up a calming space with your favorite colors and immerse yourself in the meditative process of brushstrokes on canvas. Whether you're a seasoned artist or a first-timer, abstract or landscape, the act of painting allows your mind to focus on the present moment, offering a welcome break from stressors.

Consider creating a "stress relief series" where each canvas represents a different emotion or state of mind. Experiment with blending colors and textures to visually express your feelings. The beauty of this DIY project lies not only in the finished artwork but also in the journey of self-discovery and emotional release that accompanies the process.

2: Zen in a Jar - Creating Tranquil Terrariums

Embrace the art of terrarium-making as a soothing and visually appealing DIY project. Gather a variety of plants, small stones, and decorative elements to create your own little green oasis. Terrariums are not only beautiful to look at but also serve as a reminder to nurture and care for living things, fostering a sense of responsibility and connection to nature.

Building a terrarium engages your senses in a calming way, from the soft touch of soil to the earthy fragrance of plants. Choose a glass container that suits your style, whether it's a minimalist geometric shape or a vintage glass jar. As you assemble your terrarium, let your mind wander and focus on the simple pleasures of the natural world. Placing your finished creation in a prominent spot in your home brings a touch of tranquility to your daily surroundings.

3: Mandala Magic - Meditative Coloring for Stress Relief

Discover the mesmerizing world of mandalas, intricate geometric patterns that have been used for centuries as a tool for meditation. Engaging in mandala coloring is a simple yet powerful way to calm the mind and reduce stress. Select a mandala design that resonates with you, print it out, and let the coloring begin.

The repetitive nature of coloring within the lines allows your mind to enter a state of flow, where worries take a back seat to the creative process. Experiment with different color combinations and techniques, making each mandala a unique expression of your mood. Consider framing your completed mandalas as a visual reminder of the peace you've found through this therapeutic DIY art project.

4: Blissful Beats - Homemade Stress-Relief Music Playlist

Take a different approach to DIY art by curating your stress-relief music playlist. Music has a profound impact on our emotions, and creating a personalized playlist can be a form of sonic artistry. Begin by selecting songs that resonate with feelings of calm, joy, and serenity. Whether it's classical compositions, acoustic melodies, or nature sounds, let your musical preferences guide you.

Arrange your playlist thoughtfully, considering the flow of each song and how they complement one another. As you listen, allow the music to transport you to a place of relaxation. You can even take it a step further by incorporating DIY elements, such as creating album cover art or themed playlists for different moods. Music, as a form of art, has the power to transport you and provide solace during stressful moments.

5: Stitching Serenity - The Art of Mindful Embroidery

Embark on a stitching journey with mindful embroidery as your guide. This tactile and rhythmic DIY art project allows you to create intricate designs while promoting relaxation. Select a simple pattern or let your creativity flow with free-form stitching. The repetitive nature of embroidery is a form of active meditation, calming the mind and promoting mindfulness.

Experiment with different thread colors and textures, letting your hands guide the needle in a soothing dance. Consider stitching designs that hold personal significance or convey positive affirmations. Completing an embroidery project not only leaves you with a beautiful piece of art but also a tangible representation of the patience and focus required for stress relief.

6: Journaling for Joy - Artistic Expression on Paper

Wrap up your DIY stress-relief art journey with the expressive and therapeutic practice of journaling. Unleash your thoughts, feelings, and creativity onto paper through writing, sketching, or a combination of both. A stress relief journal is a safe space for self-reflection, providing an outlet for processing emotions and celebrating small victories.

Experiment with different journaling techniques, such as gratitude journaling, where you focus on positive aspects of your life, or visual journaling, combining words and images to tell your story. Consider decorating your journal cover with DIY elements like collage or hand-drawn designs. This tangible record of your artistic and emotional journey becomes a valuable tool for self-discovery and stress management.

Conclusion: Artful Serenity - A DIY Sanctuary for Stress Relief

In conclusion, incorporating DIY art projects into your routine can be a transformative and enjoyable way to combat stress. Whether you're painting, crafting, or curating playlists, the act of creation serves as a form of self-care. Experiment with different projects, find what resonates with you, and let the therapeutic power of art bring serenity to your daily life.

HARMONY IN DESIGN: UNVEILING THE POWER OF SYMMETRY IN WALL ART DISPLAYS

Welcome to a world where balance and beauty collide in perfect harmony. In this blog post, "Harmony in Design," we unravel the captivating power of symmetry in wall art displays. From the allure of perfect proportions to the tranquility of mirrored compositions, discover how incorporating symmetry elevates your living space into a realm of aesthetic bliss. Join us on a journey where every piece of art becomes a part of a perfectly orchestrated symphony, creating an atmosphere of visual delight and timeless elegance.

Symmetry Unveiled: The Artistic Dance of Mirrored Perfection

Begin our exploration in "Symmetry Unveiled," where we delve into the concept of symmetry as the artistic dance of mirrored perfection. Symmetry, in its simplest form, refers to a balanced arrangement of elements on either side of a central axis. This timeless design principle has been celebrated across cultures and centuries for its ability to evoke a sense of order and aesthetic harmony.

Consider selecting wall art pieces that embody symmetrical balance, where each side mirrors the other. This could be achieved through geometric patterns, mirrored images, or even diptych and triptych arrangements. The allure of symmetry lies in its ability to create a sense of stability and visual order, transforming your walls into a canvas of elegant precision.

Perfect Proportions: The Allure of Balanced Compositions

Transition into the second section, "Perfect Proportions," where we explore the allure of balanced compositions. Symmetry extends beyond mere mirroring; it encompasses the meticulous consideration of proportions. Perfectly balanced compositions draw the eye in, creating a focal point that commands attention while maintaining a sense of equilibrium.

Consider incorporating wall art that embraces perfect proportions, whether through traditional artwork, framed photography, or even sculptural pieces. The beauty of perfect proportions lies in their universal appeal – they transcend trends and resonate with our innate sense of visual harmony. Explore the world of balanced compositions and witness how the allure of perfect proportions transforms your living space into a gallery of timeless elegance.

Mirrored Magic: Creating Visual Depth with Symmetry

In the third section, "Mirrored Magic," we explore how symmetry creates visual depth, adding a touch of magic to your wall art displays. Mirroring elements not only enhances the aesthetic appeal but also introduces a sense of spatial illusion. The repetition of forms on either side of the central axis tricks the eye, making your space appear larger and more expansive.

Choose wall art pieces that incorporate mirrored magic, such as reflective surfaces, repeated patterns, or even ornate frames. Mirrored symmetry introduces a subtle play of light and shadow, creating an ever-changing visual experience throughout the day. Immerse yourself in the mirrored magic of symmetry and watch as your living space becomes a dynamic showcase of visual depth and intrigue.

Asymmetry: The Artful Twist in Symmetrical Displays

Move on to "Asymmetry," where we explore the artful twist in symmetrical displays. While the focus has been on perfect mirroring so far, asymmetry introduces an element of surprise and individuality. Strategic placement of contrasting elements disrupts the traditional symmetrical order, infusing energy and dynamism into your wall art displays.

Consider incorporating asymmetrical compositions through the juxtaposition of different-sized frames, varied artwork styles, or even an intentional imbalance in the arrangement. Asymmetry adds a touch of modern flair, preventing the design from feeling too static or predictable. Explore the artful twist in symmetrical displays and witness how asymmetry injects personality and vitality into your curated gallery.

Balancing Act: Mixing Styles and Sizes in Symmetrical Galleries

Enter the fifth section, "Balancing Act," where we explore the delicate art of mixing styles and sizes in symmetrical galleries. The beauty of symmetry lies in its versatility – it accommodates diverse styles and sizes, creating a harmonious yet eclectic visual experience. Experiment with different types of wall art, from paintings and prints to sculptures and photographs.

Consider creating a symmetrical gallery wall where each piece, despite its uniqueness, contributes to the overall balance of the display. This balancing act allows you to showcase your personal style while maintaining a cohesive and visually appealing arrangement. Dive into the world of mixing styles and sizes in symmetrical galleries and witness how this curated approach transforms your walls into a captivating masterpiece.

DIY Symmetry: Crafting Personalized Wall Art Displays

In the final section, "DIY Symmetry," we explore the joy of crafting personalized wall art displays with a symmetrical touch. Unleash your creativity by designing and arranging your own symmetrical compositions. Whether through a series of handcrafted pieces or a curated collection of found objects, DIY symmetry allows you to infuse your living space with a personal touch.

Consider involving family members in DIY projects, turning the creation of symmetrical wall art into a collaborative and meaningful experience. The joy of DIY symmetry lies not only in the finished display but also in the process of self-expression and creativity. Embrace the art of crafting personalized wall art displays, where every piece becomes a reflection of your unique style and vision.

Conclusion:

As we conclude our journey through the power of symmetry in wall art displays, remember that balance is the key to visual harmony. Whether you're drawn to the mirrored perfection, perfect proportions, mirrored magic, the artful twist of asymmetry, the balancing act of mixing styles and sizes, or the joy of DIY symmetry, each section unveils a facet of the transformative power that symmetry holds in elevating your living space into a realm of aesthetic bliss.

ARTFUL ACCENTS: DRAWING ATTENTION TO YOUR PROPERTY'S BEST FEATURES

Setting the Stage with Artful Elegance

Step into a world where art becomes the star of the show, transforming your property into a captivating masterpiece. In "Artful Accents," we explore the transformative power of art as a focal point, guiding you through the process of drawing attention to your property's most exquisite features.

"The Power of First Impressions: Art at the Entryway"

In "The Power of First Impressions," we uncover the art of making a statement right from the entrance. Discover how strategically placed artworks, whether bold sculptures or vibrant installations, can create an immediate and lasting impression, setting the tone for the entire property. Explore the interplay between art and curb appeal as a dynamic duo that captures attention.

"Architectural Harmony: Integrating Art with Design"

"Architectural Harmony" explores the seamless integration of art with your property's design. Dive into the world of art that complements architectural elements, enhancing the overall aesthetic appeal. From sculptures echoing the property's lines to murals that breathe life into empty spaces, discover how art becomes an intrinsic part of your property's design narrative.

"Outdoor Elegance: Sculpting Nature with Art"

"Outdoor Elegance" takes the spotlight to the great outdoors, exploring how art can accentuate the natural beauty of your property. Delve into the world of outdoor sculptures, garden installations, and artistic landscaping that not only draw attention but create a harmonious dialogue with nature, elevating your property's allure.

"Artful Interiors: Enhancing Key Living Spaces"

"Artful Interiors" delves into the heart of your property, exploring how art can enhance key living spaces. From living rooms to dining areas, understand the art of choosing pieces that not only complement the room's function but also draw attention to architectural highlights. Discover how curated art selections can elevate the living experience for residents and guests alike.

"A View to Remember: Art and Scenic Vistas"

"A View to Remember" shifts the focus to properties with scenic vistas, exploring how art can enhance these breathtaking backdrops. Whether overlooking city skylines, mountains, or oceans, learn how to strategically position art to frame and complement these natural panoramas. Uncover the secrets to creating picturesque views that become iconic features of your property.

"Investing in Artful Value: The Impact on Property Appreciation"

"Investing in Artful Value" concludes our exploration, delving into the impact of art on property appreciation. Understand how the careful curation of art can contribute to the long-term value of your property. From attracting potential buyers to creating a distinct brand for your property, discover the financial and aesthetic rewards of making art a focal point.

ARTISTIC NOOKS: CREATING INTIMATE SPACES WITH WALL DÉCOR

Step into the world of "Artistic Nooks," where the fusion of creativity and coziness transforms ordinary spaces into intimate retreats. In this blog post, we'll explore the art of adorning nooks with wall décor, turning them into personal havens that inspire and embrace.

The Reading Corner Renaissance: Literary Escapes with Wall Art

Dive into "The Reading Corner Renaissance" and discover how art can breathe life into your book nook. From literary-themed prints to cozy seating adorned with textured tapestries, explore the myriad ways wall décor can create an atmosphere that invites you to escape into the enchanting worlds of your favorite reads. The Reading Corner Renaissance encourages you to infuse your nook with pieces that speak to your literary soul.

Consider incorporating a whimsical reading-themed wall decal or framing quotes from your favorite authors for a personalized touch.

Meditative Retreats: Serenity in Wall Décor

In "Meditative Retreats," we explore the art of transforming small corners into calming sanctuaries. Discover how serene landscapes, abstract art, or mandala-inspired pieces can create a meditative atmosphere. Meditative Retreats invites you to curate a nook that provides a visual escape, fostering moments of tranquility and mindfulness in your daily routine.

Consider using soft, neutral colors in your wall décor to enhance the calming effect of your meditative nook.

Artisanal Workspaces: Inspiring Creativity in Small Corners

"Artisanal Workspaces" unveils the potential of nooks as creative hubs. Whether you're into crafting, writing, or sketching, explore how curated wall art can turn compact corners into artisanal retreats. Artisanal Workspaces inspires you to surround your creative nook with pieces that fuel inspiration and enhance your artistic endeavors.

Consider adding a corkboard wall for displaying inspiration boards, sketches, and motivational quotes, creating a dynamic and ever-evolving space.

Musical Havens: Harmonizing Walls with Melodies

In "Musical Havens," we harmonize walls with melodies, transforming nooks into spaces that celebrate the magic of music. From vinyl record displays to musical note wall decals, discover how wall art can resonate with your love for sound. Musical Havens encourages you to curate a nook that not only echoes with your favorite tunes but visually celebrates the artistry of music.

Consider using acoustic panels or sound-absorbing wall art to enhance the acoustics of your musical haven.

Nature-Inspired Alcoves: Bringing the Outdoors In

"Nature-Inspired Alcoves" invites you to blur the lines between indoors and outdoors. Explore how wall art featuring botanical prints, landscapes, or nature-inspired patterns can turn small corners into verdant retreats. Nature-Inspired Alcoves encourages you to embrace the calming influence of nature within the confines of your home.

Consider complementing your nature-themed wall décor with potted plants or succulents to create a seamless connection to the outdoors.

Gallery of Memories: Nooks as Personal Time Capsules

In our final section, "Gallery of Memories," we explore the role of nooks as personal time capsules. Discover how family photos, travel mementos, and nostalgic wall art can turn small corners into intimate galleries of your life's journey. Gallery of Memories encourages you to curate a nook that not only envelops you in the present but also tells the story of your past.

Consider creating a gallery wall in your nook, combining photos, memorabilia, and artwork for a unique and sentimental touch.

Conclusion:

In "Artistic Nooks: Creating Intimate Spaces with Wall Décor," we've embarked on a journey to redefine small corners as artistic havens. From reading retreats to musical alcoves, each nook tells a unique story. Let this blog post inspire you to transform overlooked spaces into cherished corners, where the fusion of art and intimacy cultivates a sense of personal sanctuary.

GREEN GALLERY: ECO-FRIENDLY WALL ART OPTIONS FOR SUSTAINABLE PROPERTY VALUE

Sustainably Shaping Spaces with Eco-Friendly Wall Art

Welcome to the future of interior design where sustainability meets aesthetics. In "Green Gallery," we explore the diverse realm of eco-friendly wall art options that not only enhance the visual appeal of spaces but also contribute to sustainable property value. Join us on a journey through innovative and environmentally conscious art choices that make a positive impact on both your living space and the planet.

"Nature's Palette: Botanical Wall Art for Biophilic Bliss"

In "Nature's Palette," we dive into the world of botanical wall art, celebrating the beauty of nature within your living spaces. Explore the serene allure of botanical prints, moss walls, and sustainably sourced wooden art that brings the outdoors inside. Discover how these eco-friendly options not only enhance the aesthetics of a property but also foster a sense of well-being and connection to nature, creating a harmonious environment that can positively influence property values.

Immerse yourself in the calming embrace of nature's palette and its impact on sustainable property value.

"Recycled Revelry: Artistic Creations from Upcycled Materials"

In "Recycled Revelry," we unravel the artistic possibilities of upcycled materials, turning discarded items into stunning pieces of wall art. Explore how artists and designers are creatively repurposing materials like reclaimed wood, metal, and plastics to craft unique and eco-friendly art installations. Delve into the world of sustainable sculptures and wall hangings that not only tell a story of renewal but also contribute to a circular economy, adding an element of conscious creativity to your property.

Witness the magic of recycled revelry and how upcycled art can be a sustainable asset for your living spaces.

"Solar-Powered Statements: Harnessing Energy for Artistic Illumination"

In "Solar-Powered Statements," we explore the integration of solar technology into wall art, transforming your space into a beacon of sustainable design. Discover the artful possibilities of solar-powered LED installations, creating dynamic and energy-efficient statements that illuminate your property. Learn how these eco-friendly options not only reduce energy consumption but also add a futuristic and visually striking element to your walls, enhancing both the aesthetic and sustainable appeal of your living space.

Experience the brilliance of solar-powered statements and their impact on sustainable property value.

"Canvas and Cork: Sustainable Materials for Artistic Expression"

In "Canvas and Cork," we shift our focus to sustainable materials that redefine artistic expression. Explore the versatility of cork as a canvas for eco-friendly wall art, offering not only a unique texture but also sustainable harvesting practices. Dive into the world of corkboard murals, paintings, and wall coverings that contribute to a healthier indoor environment while making a positive statement about your commitment to sustainable living. Uncover the artistry of canvas and cork and how these materials are elevating the green quotient of modern interiors.

Embrace the sustainable elegance of canvas and cork and witness their transformative impact on property value.

"Living Walls: Verdant Vertical Gardens for Sustainable Luxury"

In "Living Walls," we embark on a journey into the realm of verdant vertical gardens, turning walls into lush, sustainable masterpieces. Explore the beauty of living art installations that incorporate real plants and moss, not only purifying the air but also creating a refreshing and vibrant atmosphere. Learn how living walls contribute to sustainability by improving indoor air quality and providing insulation, making them a unique and impactful addition to any property seeking a touch of green luxury.

Immerse yourself in the sustainable opulence of living walls and their contribution to property value.

"Eco-Conscious Investments: The Long-Term Impact of Sustainable Wall Art"

In "Eco-Conscious Investments," we discuss the long-term impact of sustainable wall art on property value. Understand how eco-friendly choices can contribute to a property's desirability and market appeal. Explore case studies highlighting the financial benefits of sustainable investments, from increased energy efficiency to a positive perception among eco-conscious buyers. Gain insights into the growing demand for sustainable features in real estate and how embracing eco-friendly wall art can position your property as a forward-thinking and valuable investment.

Unlock the secrets of eco-conscious investments and witness the lasting impact on sustainable property value.

NATURE'S GALLERY: ELEVATING YOUR SPACE WITH NATURE-INSPIRED WALL ART

Step into the enchanting world of nature-inspired wall art, where the beauty of the outdoors is brought indoors to transform your living space. In this blog post, we'll explore the magic of integrating nature-themed artworks, capturing the serenity and vibrancy of the natural world. From botanical prints to landscapes, join us on a journey of creating a harmonious connection with nature within the confines of your home.

The Symphony of Greens: Embracing Botanical Bliss in Wall Art:

Let's begin our exploration with the symphony of greens, where botanical bliss takes center stage in nature-inspired wall art. Embrace the freshness and vitality of the outdoors by adorning your walls with botanical prints and illustrations. Choose artwork featuring leaves, flowers, or entire plant compositions that bring a touch of the garden into your living space.

Botanical wall art is incredibly versatile, suiting various interior styles from modern to traditional. Create a gallery wall with an array of botanical prints or let a single large botanical artwork become a statement piece. The symphony of greens transforms your home into a natural sanctuary, where the vibrancy and life of plants breathe freshness into every room.

Landscape Escapes: Capturing the Majesty of Nature on Canvas:

Transport yourself to serene landscapes with wall art that captures the majesty of nature on canvas. Whether it's a sweeping mountain vista, a tranquil lakeside scene, or a sunset over the ocean, landscape-inspired artworks bring the beauty of the outdoors into your home. These pieces not only add visual interest but also evoke a sense of calm and wonder.

Consider selecting artwork that resonates with your favorite natural landscapes or holds sentimental value. Large landscape prints can create a focal point in a living room or bedroom, instantly transforming the ambiance. The escape to nature through landscape-inspired wall art allows you to create a retreat within your own home, where the wonders of the great outdoors become a part of your everyday surroundings.

The Whimsy of Wildlife: Adding Playfulness with Animal-Inspired Art:

Infuse a touch of whimsy into your space with wildlife-inspired wall art that brings the charm of animals into your home. From graceful deer to majestic elephants, animal-themed artworks add playfulness and character to your walls. Consider framed prints, canvases, or even metal sculptures that capture the essence of your favorite creatures.

Create themed arrangements, such as a gallery wall dedicated to wildlife or a series of smaller animal prints dispersed throughout the space. The whimsy of wildlife-inspired art goes beyond aesthetics; it creates a sense of connection with the animal kingdom, fostering a lighthearted and delightful atmosphere in your home.

Seascapes and Shorelines: Channeling Tranquility with Coastal Art:

Bring the calming influence of the coast into your living space with seascapes and shoreline-inspired wall art. Coastal art evokes a sense of tranquility, making it ideal for creating a serene and relaxed atmosphere. Choose artwork featuring ocean views, beach scenes, or coastal elements like seashells and driftwood.

Consider a mix of blue tones and sandy neutrals to capture the essence of the seaside. Seascapes can be featured prominently in living rooms, bedrooms, or even bathrooms, creating a coastal retreat within your home. The soothing influence of coastal art allows you to escape the hustle and bustle of daily life and immerse yourself in the calming rhythms of the ocean.

Abstract Nature: Exploring the Artistic Essence of the Outdoors:

Dive into the artistic essence of the outdoors with abstract nature-inspired wall art. Abstract pieces that draw inspiration from natural elements, such as water, air, or flora, offer a unique and visually intriguing way to bring nature into your home. Explore a diverse range of colors, shapes, and textures that mimic the complexity and beauty of the natural world.

Abstract nature art allows for personal interpretation and adds a contemporary touch to your space. Whether it's a vibrant burst of color reminiscent of a sunset or the fluid movement of lines reflecting the wind, abstract nature art brings an artistic and dynamic dimension to your walls. Embrace the creative energy of the outdoors through abstract interpretations that invite contemplation and exploration.

DIY Nature: Infusing Your Personal Touch into Nature-Inspired Wall Art:

In the final section, let's explore the joy of infusing your personal touch into nature-inspired wall art through DIY projects. Whether you're a budding artist or a craft enthusiast, creating your own nature-themed artworks adds a unique and intimate layer to your home decor. Consider painting a canvas with your favorite natural elements, pressing botanical specimens into frames, or creating a collage of nature photographs.

DIY nature art not only allows for customization but also brings a sense of accomplishment and personal connection to your living space. Invite friends or family to join in the creative process, turning it into a shared experience. The DIY approach to nature-inspired wall art ensures that your walls become a canvas for your own creativity, reflecting your unique perspective on the beauty of the outdoors.

Conclusion:

As we conclude our journey through nature's gallery and the art of bringing the outdoors in, remember that nature-inspired wall art is more than decoration – it's a gateway to serenity, wonder, and personal expression. From the symphony of greens to landscape escapes.

SHAPE YOUR SPACE: EMBRACING TRENDY GEOMETRIC WALL ART IDEAS

Welcome to the world of geometric shapes and patterns, where the power of lines and angles transforms your walls into contemporary masterpieces. In this blog post, we'll dive into the trendy realm of geometric wall art ideas, exploring how these bold and dynamic designs can add flair, sophistication, and a touch of modernity to your living space. Join us on a journey of exploring shapes that go beyond the ordinary, infusing your home with a sense of style that is both current and timeless.

The Geometry of Expression: Unleashing Creativity with Abstract Geometric Art:

Let's start our exploration by unleashing creativity through abstract geometric art. Abstract shapes and patterns provide a canvas for expression, allowing you to play with form, color, and composition. Choose bold triangles, intersecting lines, or circular motifs that resonate with your style. Abstract geometric art becomes a focal point, sparking conversations and adding a dynamic energy to your living space.

Experiment with different color palettes – from monochromatic schemes for a minimalist vibe to vibrant hues that make a bold statement. The beauty of abstract geometric art lies in its ability to adapt to various interior styles, whether it's a sleek and modern apartment or a cozy bohemian abode. Embrace the geometry of expression, and let your walls become a gallery of your unique artistic sensibility.

Symmetry and Harmony: Elevating Elegance with Geometric Patterns:

Enter the realm of symmetry and harmony as we explore the elegance of geometric patterns. Whether it's classic chevron, herringbone, or intricate lattice designs, geometric patterns bring a sense of order and sophistication to your walls. Consider creating an accent wall with geometric wallpaper or hanging framed prints that showcase repetitive shapes in a harmonious arrangement.

Symmetry in geometric patterns creates a visual balance that appeals to the eye, making it an ideal choice for those who appreciate a refined and orderly aesthetic. Explore monochrome patterns for a timeless look or experiment with contrasting colors to add vibrancy to your space. Symmetry and harmony in geometric patterns elevate the elegance of your home, turning walls into works of art that exude a sense of balance and style.

3D Illusions: Adding Depth with Geometric Wall Sculptures:

Step into the third dimension with the trend of 3D illusions created by geometric wall sculptures. These dynamic pieces add depth, texture, and a touch of the avant-garde to your living space. Geometric sculptures can range from metal designs that cast intriguing shadows to layered wooden creations that invite tactile exploration. Consider placing these sculptures in areas where light can play with the shadows, enhancing the overall visual impact.

Explore the play between positive and negative space, where geometric shapes seem to leap from the wall. Geometric wall sculptures not only add a contemporary edge but also contribute to the sensory experience of your home. Embrace the trend of 3D illusions, and let your walls become a sculptural canvas that captivates and intrigues.

Color Block Brilliance: Making a Statement with Bold Geometric Colors:

Make a bold statement by infusing color block brilliance into your space with vibrant geometric shapes. Color blocking involves combining contrasting or complementary colors in large, solid sections, creating a striking visual impact. Geometric shapes become the vehicle for this dynamic expression of color, turning your walls into a lively and modern canvas.

Consider color blocking an entire wall or creating a mural with oversized geometric shapes. The key is to choose colors that resonate with your personality and the overall theme of your space. From jewel tones that exude luxury to playful pastels that evoke a sense of whimsy, color block brilliance adds personality and vibrancy to your home. Embrace the trend, and let your walls become a celebration of bold geometric colors.

Mosaic Magic: Crafting Intricate Designs with Geometric Tiles:

Experience the magic of mosaics as we delve into crafting intricate designs with geometric tiles. Geometric tiles allow you to create patterns that range from subtle to intricate, adding a touch of timeless charm to your walls. Whether it's a backsplash in the kitchen, an accent wall in the bathroom, or a decorative element in the living room, geometric tiles offer endless possibilities for creative expression.

Experiment with different tile shapes – hexagons, diamonds, or subway tiles – and play with arrangements to create unique geometric patterns. Consider a monochrome palette for a classic look or introduce a mix of colors for a more eclectic vibe. Mosaic magic transforms your walls into a tapestry of geometric elegance, where every tile contributes to the overall visual narrative of your space.

Gallery of Geometric Memories: Personalizing Spaces with Custom Art Arrangements:

Conclude our journey by creating a gallery of geometric memories, where custom art arrangements become a personal expression of your style. Mix and match geometric prints, paintings, and sculptures to curate a gallery wall that tells a story unique to you. Arrange the pieces in a way that reflects your taste, memories, and the geometry of your life.

Consider incorporating personal photographs, DIY geometric projects, or custom artworks that hold sentimental value. The gallery of geometric memories goes beyond trends, creating a space that is intimately yours. Experiment with different sizes, shapes, and textures to add a dynamic dimension

 to your gallery wall. Personalizing spaces with custom art arrangements allows you to turn your walls into a visual autobiography that evolves with you over time.

Conclusion:

As we conclude our journey through the world of geometric shapes and patterns, remember that the possibilities are as vast as the angles and lines that inspire these designs. From abstract expressions and symmetrical elegance to 3D illusions and color block brilliance, let your walls become a canvas where geometry meets creativity. Embrace the trendy world of geometric wall art ideas, and shape your space with a touch of contemporary flair.

WHIMSICAL WATERCOLORS: TRANSFORMING SPACES WITH DELICATE ART

Welcome to the enchanting world of "Whimsical Watercolors," where the delicate strokes of this timeless medium breathe life into your living spaces. In this blog post, we embark on a journey through six sections that explore the captivating charm of watercolor art. From its versatile applications to the soothing palette, discover how whimsical watercolors can soften and elevate the ambiance of your home.

The Magic of Watercolors: An Introduction to the Medium

In "The Magic of Watercolors," we delve into the unique characteristics that make watercolors a beloved choice for artists and art enthusiasts alike. Explore the transparent nature of watercolor pigments, allowing the underlying paper texture to shine through. Learn how artists can achieve a wide range of effects, from ethereal washes to intricate details, creating a sense of fluidity and spontaneity that defines the magic of watercolors.

Consider incorporating watercolor art into your home to capture the medium's expressive and dreamlike qualities. From abstract pieces to detailed botanical illustrations, let the magic of watercolors set the tone for the whimsical journey ahead.

Softening Spaces: The Gentle Impact of Watercolor Art

In "Softening Spaces," we unravel the gentle yet impactful influence of watercolor art on the overall atmosphere of a room. Discover how the soft, muted tones of watercolors create a calming and tranquil environment. Explore the versatility of watercolor art in adapting to various interior design styles, from minimalist and contemporary to shabby chic and bohemian.

Consider adorning your bedroom with a large watercolor landscape, bringing a sense of serenity to your personal retreat. Softening Spaces invites you to embrace the subtle yet transformative power of watercolor art in creating an inviting and harmonious home.

Botanical Elegance: Watercolor Florals and Nature Scenes

In "Botanical Elegance," we celebrate the timeless beauty of watercolor florals and nature scenes. Explore how artists use delicate brushstrokes to capture the intricacies of flowers, leaves, and landscapes. Learn how watercolor botanical art can bring a touch of nature indoors, infusing your space with the elegance of blooming flowers and lush greenery.

Consider creating a gallery wall featuring a collection of watercolor botanical prints to establish a harmonious connection between art and nature in your home. Botanical Elegance encourages you to let the beauty of watercolor florals bloom within your living spaces.

Abstract Whispers: Expressive Freedom in Watercolor Abstraction

In "Abstract Whispers," we explore the expressive freedom found in watercolor abstraction. Delve into the world of spontaneous brushstrokes, vibrant color palettes, and ethereal compositions that define abstract watercolor art. Learn how artists use this medium to convey emotions, thoughts, and abstract concepts through a language of color and form.

Consider incorporating abstract watercolor pieces into your living room to add a dynamic and thought-provoking element to the space. Abstract Whispers invites you to embrace the artistic spontaneity and interpretative nature of abstract watercolor art.

Whimsy and Fantasy: Watercolor in Children's Spaces

In "Whimsy and Fantasy," we discover the enchanting role watercolor art plays in creating magical and imaginative environments, especially in children's spaces. Explore how soft pastels and dreamy watercolor illustrations can transport young minds to whimsical realms. Learn how watercolor art contributes to a nurturing and creative atmosphere for children to explore and grow.

Consider decorating a nursery or playroom with watercolor animal prints, fairy-tale scenes, or personalized watercolor name art. Whimsy and Fantasy invite you to infuse a touch of magic into your little one's world with the delicate allure of watercolor art.

DIY Watercolor Adventures: Unleashing Your Inner Artist

In "DIY Watercolor Adventures," we encourage you to unleash your inner artist and embark on a creative journey with watercolors. Discover simple and enjoyable DIY watercolor projects that cater to all skill levels. From creating personalized greeting cards to experimenting with abstract techniques, embrace the joy of hands-on watercolor exploration.

Consider hosting a watercolor painting session with friends or family to foster creativity and camaraderie. DIY Watercolor Adventures invites you to not only appreciate watercolor art but to actively engage in the artistic process and discover the artist within you.

Conclusion:

As we conclude our exploration of "Whimsical Watercolors," let the delicate strokes and enchanting hues of this timeless medium inspire you to transform your living spaces into havens of creativity and tranquility. Whether you're drawn to the magic of watercolors, the softening impact on spaces, botanical elegance, abstract whispers, whimsy and fantasy, or DIY watercolor adventures, each section unfolds a chapter in the captivating story of watercolor art.

COLORFUL SYMPHONY: MASTERING THE ART OF CONTRAST AND HARMONY IN WALL ART DISPLAYS

Welcome to the vibrant world of wall art, where colors dance together in a harmonious symphony or stand out boldly in striking contrast. In this blog post, we'll explore the art of balancing colors in wall art displays, guiding you through the intricacies of creating visual masterpieces that evoke emotions, tell stories, and transform your living space. From the subtle interplay of harmonious tones to the bold contrast that commands attention, join us on a journey through the colorful spectrum of wall art.

The Color Palette Palette: Choosing the Right Tones for Your Space

Embark on our journey with "The Color Palette Palette," where we dive into the crucial step of choosing the right tones for your wall art. Consider the existing color scheme of your room, the mood you want to evoke, and the overall aesthetic you're aiming for. Harmonious wall art integrates seamlessly with the surroundings, enhancing the existing palette without overpowering it.

Explore the possibilities of monochromatic schemes that bring depth and sophistication, or analogous colors that create a soothing and cohesive atmosphere. Choosing the right color palette sets the stage for a visual experience that is not only aesthetically pleasing but also emotionally resonant. Uncover the secrets of selecting tones that create a harmonious backdrop for your wall art journey.

Bold Statements: The Power of High-Contrast Wall Art

Transition into "Bold Statements," where we explore the impactful realm of high-contrast wall art. For those who crave drama and attention, high-contrast displays become the focal point of a room, demanding admiration and sparking conversations. Consider pairings of complementary colors or the stark juxtaposition of black and white for a timeless and powerful effect.

Experiment with bold patterns, abstract designs, or vibrant hues that pop against neutral backgrounds. High-contrast wall art is not just about color; it's about making a statement and infusing energy into your space. Dive into the world of bold contrasts and discover how your walls can become canvases that command attention and leave a lasting impression.

Color Psychology: Eliciting Emotions Through Wall Art

In the third section, "Color Psychology," we unravel the emotional impact of colors in wall art displays. Each color carries a unique psychological weight, influencing mood, perception, and even behavior. Explore the soothing effects of blues and greens for spaces of relaxation, the warmth of yellows and oranges for areas of sociability, or the passion evoked by reds and purples in intimate settings.

Consider the emotional resonance you want your wall art to convey and choose colors that align with those sentiments. Whether it's a serene bedroom retreat, a lively living room, or a focused home office, understanding the psychology of colors allows you to curate an environment that speaks to the soul. Delve into the emotional tapestry that colors weave on your walls.

Creating Flow: Integrating Multiple Pieces with Cohesive Colors

Move on to "Creating Flow," where we explore the art of integrating multiple pieces into a cohesive display. Whether you're curating a gallery wall or arranging a series of pieces, maintaining color harmony ensures that your collection feels like a unified composition rather than a random assortment. Consider a common color thread that ties the pieces together, creating a visual flow that guides the eye seamlessly from one artwork to the next.

Experiment with different sizes, styles, and subjects while keeping the color palette consistent. Creating flow in your wall art display not only elevates the visual appeal of each individual piece but also transforms your entire wall into a curated masterpiece. Discover the art of storytelling through a harmonious color journey that unfolds across your walls.

Texture and Tone: Adding Depth to Wall Art Displays

Enter the fifth section, "Texture and Tone," where we explore the dimensionality brought forth by varying textures and tones in wall art. Beyond color, the interplay of light and shadow, matte and gloss, adds depth and richness to your display. Consider mixing materials like canvas, metal, and wood to create a tactile experience that engages both the eyes and the sense of touch.

Experiment with tonal variations within a single color family to create subtle contrasts that add nuance to your wall art. The marriage of texture and tone transforms your walls into a sensory canvas, inviting exploration and creating an immersive experience for those who encounter your art. Dive into the tactile realm and discover how texture and tone elevate your wall displays to new heights.

The Art of Balance: Fine-Tuning Your Wall Art Ensemble

In the final section, "The Art of Balance," we unravel the importance of fine-tuning your wall art ensemble for the perfect balance. Achieving harmony doesn't mean every piece has to match; it's about finding equilibrium in the overall composition. Step back, assess the visual weight of each element, and adjust accordingly.

Consider the spacing between pieces, the arrangement on the wall, and the overall visual impact. The art of balance ensures that no single piece overwhelms the ensemble, creating a cohesive and visually pleasing display. Fine-tune your wall art ensemble to achieve a delicate equilibrium that transforms your walls into a curated masterpiece.

Conclusion:

As we conclude our colorful journey through the intricacies of wall art, remember that the art of contrast and harmony is about more than just color. From choosing the right tones and making bold statements to understanding color psychology, creating flow, embracing texture and tone, and fine-tuning balance, each section

has illuminated a facet of the vibrant tapestry that wall art weaves in your living space. Whether you opt for harmonious blends that soothe the soul or bold contrasts that make a statement, the key lies in understanding the impact each color and texture brings to your walls.

PAINTING WITH EMOTION: DECODING THE SCIENCE OF COLOR THEORY IN ART

Color isn't just a visual feast for the eyes; it's a language that speaks to our emotions and perceptions. In this exploration, we'll dive into the captivating world of color theory in art, unraveling the science behind the choices artists make and the impact these choices have on our emotional experiences. Join me on this colorful journey as we decode the secrets behind the artistic symphony of hues.

1: The Basics of Color Theory: A Palette of Possibilities

Let's start our journey by laying the foundation with the basics of color theory. The color wheel, a visual representation of the relationships between colors, is our map in this vibrant terrain. Primary colors—red, blue, and yellow—are the building blocks from which all other colors are created. Secondary colors emerge by mixing these primaries, and tertiary colors add nuance to the spectrum. Understanding these relationships provides artists with a palette of possibilities to evoke specific emotions and create harmonious compositions.

As we explore the color wheel, consider the emotions associated with different colors. Reds may evoke passion or energy, while blues convey calmness and serenity. Artists use this knowledge strategically, choosing colors that resonate with the intended emotional impact of their work. It's not just about pretty pictures; it's about crafting an emotional narrative through the careful orchestration of colors on the canvas.

2: Warm Hues, Cool Vibes: The Emotional Language of Colors

In this section, we'll delve into the emotional language of warm and cool colors. Warm hues—reds, oranges, yellows—tend to evoke feelings of energy, warmth, and excitement. Think of a fiery sunset or a cozy fireplace. On the flip side, cool colors—blues, greens, purples—convey calmness, serenity, and a sense of distance. Picture a tranquil ocean or a misty forest. Artists leverage this emotional spectrum to communicate with viewers on a subconscious level, creating an immersive experience that goes beyond the visual.

Consider how artists like Vincent van Gogh used warm yellows to infuse his "Sunflowers" with vibrancy and energy, or how Monet's cool blues captured the serene reflections in his "Water Lilies." The choice between warm and cool colors isn't arbitrary; it's a deliberate decision that shapes the emotional landscape of the artwork, inviting viewers to feel the temperature of the scene.

3: Contrasting Harmonies: Exploring Complementary Colors

Complementary colors, found opposite each other on the color wheel, create vibrant and dynamic visual experiences. This section explores how artists use contrasting harmonies to make colors pop and create visual tension. The classic pairings of red and green, blue and orange, or yellow and purple draw attention and inject energy into a composition. Artists masterfully employ these combinations to guide the viewer's eye and enhance the impact of their work.

Consider how the use of complementary colors in Edvard Munch's "The Scream" intensifies the emotional turmoil, with the vivid blue contrasting the fiery orange tones. This deliberate clash creates a visual tension that mirrors the psychological distress depicted in the painting. Understanding the power of complementary colors allows artists to play with contrasts and elevate the emotional resonance of their creations.

4: Analogous Allure: Creating Subtle Harmony

In this section, we explore the world of analogous color schemes, where hues sit next to each other on the color wheel. Analogous combinations create a sense of harmony and cohesion, making them ideal for conveying subtlety and unity. Artists often use analogous colors to evoke specific moods or create a tranquil atmosphere. Whether it's a range of blues and greens in a seascape or warm reds and oranges in a desert sunset, analogous color schemes allow for nuanced storytelling. Analogous harmony doesn't scream for attention like complementary contrasts; instead, it whispers a cohesive narrative. Consider the soothing effect of Claude Monet's "Woman with a Parasol," where various shades of blue and green create a peaceful ambiance. Analogous color schemes provide artists with a gentle brush to paint subtle emotions and guide viewers through a harmonious visual experience.

5: The Power of Monochrome: Shades of Emotion

Monochrome doesn't mean monotony; it's a powerful tool for artists to explore the depth of emotion within a limited color range. In this section, we'll unravel the nuances of monochromatic color schemes, where variations in lightness and darkness within a single color family create visual interest. The grayscale of black and white or the sepia tones of a vintage photograph offer artists a canvas to experiment with contrast, mood, and emotional intensity.

Artists like Georgia O'Keeffe mastered the use of monochrome, employing shades of red to evoke passion and intensity in her iconic flower paintings. Monochromatic schemes allow artists to focus on the subtleties of form and texture, emphasizing the emotional power of a single color family. It's a testament to the versatility of color theory, showing that even within a monochromatic palette, emotions can resonate profoundly.

6: Contemporary Color Trends: From Pixel to Palette

Our journey concludes by exploring how color theory adapts to contemporary trends, especially in the digital age. This section delves into the impact of technology on color choices, considering how screens, pixels, and digital mediums influence the way artists approach color. From the vibrant palettes of digital art to the subdued tones of minimalist design, contemporary color trends reflect the intersection of traditional theory and modern technology.

Consider the bold, saturated colors in digital illustrations or the gradient hues seen in modern web design. The digital canvas opens up new possibilities for artists to experiment with color, pushing the boundaries of traditional theory. As we navigate this section, we'll witness the evolution of color choices in response to the ever-changing landscape of artistic expression.

NAVIGATING THE DIGITAL CANVAS: A FRIENDLY GUIDE TO SUCCESSFUL ONLINE ART PURCHASES

In the vibrant world of online art buying, the digital canvas is your gateway to a myriad of creative treasures. This friendly guide offers tips and insights to ensure that your online art purchase is not just a transaction but a delightful journey into the realm of artistic discovery.

The Art of Browsing: Navigating Online Galleries with Finesse

Browsing through online galleries is like strolling through a virtual art fair, and the art of navigating these digital spaces requires finesse. This section provides friendly tips on refining your search, utilizing filters effectively, and exploring curated collections. By honing your browsing skills, you can unearth hidden gems that align with your artistic preferences and add a personal touch to your collection.

Transitioning seamlessly between genres and styles, this section encourages art enthusiasts to embrace the adventure of discovery, allowing the digital canvas to unfold a myriad of artistic possibilities.

Beyond Pixels: Understanding Art Descriptions and Details

When buying art online, the screen becomes your portal to creativity, but understanding the details is crucial. This section guides you through the importance of reading art descriptions, understanding dimensions, and paying attention to framing details. Friendly insights on deciphering artistic intent, medium specifics, and the story behind each piece ensure that you make informed choices that resonate with your artistic sensibilities.

Just as a magnifying glass reveals intricate details in a painting, this section empowers you to go beyond pixels, appreciating the nuances that make each artwork unique. The journey into understanding art details transforms online browsing into a curated experience.

Virtual Viewing Rooms: Embracing the Online Exhibition Experience

Online art platforms often offer virtual viewing rooms, providing a simulated gallery experience from the comfort of your space. This section explores the friendly dynamics of embracing virtual exhibitions, offering tips on navigating 3D spaces, attending online openings, and interacting with artworks in a digital setting. By immersing yourself in these virtual environments, you not only preview the scale and context of artworks but also gain a sense of the artist's intended presentation.

Transitioning seamlessly from one virtual room to another, this section encourages art enthusiasts to savor the digital exhibition experience, transforming online art buying into a dynamic and interactive journey.

Connecting with Artists: The Art of Virtual Studio Visits

In the online art world, connecting with artists is not limited to physical studio visits; virtual encounters provide unique opportunities for engagement. This section guides you through the art of virtual studio visits, offering tips on participating in artist talks, following artists on social media, and exploring behind-the-scenes content. By establishing a connection with artists, you not only gain insights into their creative process but also contribute to a more personalized and meaningful art-buying experience.

Just as a face-to-face conversation with an artist adds depth to your understanding of their work, this section encourages art enthusiasts to embrace the digital dialogue, fostering connections that go beyond the confines of the online platform.

Secure Transactions: Ensuring a Safe and Trustworthy Purchase

Ensuring secure transactions is paramount when buying art online. This section provides friendly advice on verifying the legitimacy of online platforms, understanding payment options, and confirming shipping and return policies. By prioritizing secure transactions, you can approach online art buying with confidence, knowing that your purchases are protected and your investment is in safe hands.

Navigating the digital payment landscape with ease, this section encourages art enthusiasts to focus on the joy of acquiring art, free from concerns about the security of their transactions.

Unboxing the Experience: Reveling in the Arrival of Your Art

The climax of the online art buying journey is the arrival of your chosen piece. This section offers tips on unboxing your art, inspecting it for any damages, and celebrating the moment. Friendly insights on creating a dedicated space for your new acquisition and sharing the unboxing experience with the artist and the online community add a touch of communal joy to your art-buying adventure.

As you unwrap your carefully packaged artwork, this section invites you to revel in the tangible experience, transforming the digital transaction into a memorable and delightful moment of artistic connection.

BRUSHING RAINBOWS: NURTURING YOUNG PICASSOS WITH CREATIVE ART PROJECTS FOR KIDS

Introducing children to the world of art is like unlocking a treasure chest of imagination. In this guide, we'll explore an array of fun and engaging art projects designed to ignite the creative spark in young minds. From colorful masterpieces to whimsical sculptures, these projects aim to make the world of art a magical and accessible space for kids to express themselves.

Rainbow Explosion: Vibrant Watercolor Creations

Kickstarting our art adventure is the "Rainbow Explosion" project, where kids can explore the mesmerizing world of watercolors. Provide them with a palette of vibrant watercolors, brushes, and sturdy paper, and watch as their imagination takes flight. Encourage them to blend colors, experiment with brush strokes, and create a kaleidoscope of hues. Whether it's a landscape, abstract shapes, or a fantasy world, this project not only hones their artistic skills but also introduces them to the joy of color exploration.

As they splash and blend colors, kids learn about color mixing, fine-tune their motor skills, and experience the sheer delight of creating something uniquely theirs. The "Rainbow Explosion" project is not just about the final artwork; it's a journey of self-expression that unfolds with every stroke of the brush.

Cardboard Kingdom: Building 3D Sculptures

In this section, we dive into the "Cardboard Kingdom," a project that transforms ordinary cardboard into a realm of three-dimensional wonders. Collect old cardboard boxes, scissors, glue, and let the kids embark on a journey of sculptural creation. From castles and animals to spaceships and robots, the possibilities are endless. This project not only introduces them to the world of sculpture but also encourages them to envision and construct their own miniature worlds.

The "Cardboard Kingdom" project fosters creativity, problem-solving, and spatial awareness. As kids piece together their cardboard creations, they learn about form, structure, and the joy of turning everyday materials into extraordinary works of art. It's a project that transcends the flat canvas, inviting kids to think in multiple dimensions and bring their imaginative ideas to life.

Nature's Canvas: Pressed Flower Art

In the "Nature's Canvas" project, we bring the outdoors into the realm of art. Encourage kids to explore their surroundings, collect flowers, leaves, and other natural treasures, and embark on a journey of pressed flower art. With the simple technique of pressing flowers between pages of a heavy book, kids can create stunning compositions on paper or even make personalized greeting cards.

This project not only introduces kids to the beauty of nature but also teaches them about patience and observation. As they arrange the pressed flowers into artistic patterns, they learn about composition and develop an appreciation for the delicate details found in the world around them. "Nature's Canvas" is a delightful project that merges art and nature, fostering a connection between creativity and the great outdoors.

Silhouette Stories: Exploring Shadow Art

In the "Silhouette Stories" project, kids delve into the enchanting world of shadow art. Set up a light source, have them create simple cut-out shapes, and watch as their imaginations cast magical shadows on a blank surface. Whether it's animals, people, or imaginary creatures, this project encourages storytelling through the captivating interplay of light and shadow.

The "Silhouette Stories" project not only introduces kids to the concept of negative space and silhouettes but also sparks their narrative skills. As they experiment with different cut-out shapes and arrange them to tell a visual story, they explore the dynamic relationship between light and form. It's a project that invites kids to engage in storytelling not just through words but through the mesmerizing language of shadows.

Roll and Paint: Exploring Texture with DIY Rollers

Texture takes center stage in the "Roll and Paint" project, where kids create their own DIY texture rollers. Using materials like bubble wrap, corrugated cardboard, and rubber bands, they can craft unique rollers that add depth and dimension to their artwork. Rollers in hand, they can then explore the fascinating world of texture by applying paint to their rollers and transferring the patterns onto paper.

This project not only introduces kids to the tactile element of art but also encourages them to think about the variety of textures found in the world around them. From smooth surfaces to bumpy textures, the "Roll and Paint" project is a hands-on exploration of the multi-sensory experience of creating art. It's an opportunity for kids to engage with materials in a new way and discover the rich world of textures at their fingertips.

Art Around the World: Cultural Exploration through Creativity

In our final section, we embark on a cultural journey with the "Art Around the World" project. This project encourages kids to explore diverse artistic traditions from different countries. Whether it's creating Japanese cherry blossom paintings, African mud cloth-inspired patterns, or Australian Aboriginal dot paintings, kids can immerse themselves in the rich tapestry of global art.

"Art Around the World" not only introduces kids to

various artistic techniques but also fosters an appreciation for cultural diversity. As they create art inspired by different regions, they gain insights into the vibrant histories and traditions that shape the world of art. This project is a celebration of creativity as a universal language that transcends borders and connects us all.

ECO-FRIENDLY ART: SUSTAINABLE CHOICES FOR A GREENER HOME

Step into a world where art meets sustainability. In "Eco-Friendly Art: Sustainable Choices for a Greener Home," we explore how creative expression and environmental consciousness can coexist harmoniously. From the materials used to the impact on the planet, discover how your art choices can contribute to a more sustainable, eco-friendly lifestyle.

Green Canvas: Sustainable Painting Materials

In "Green Canvas," we embark on a journey to discover sustainable painting materials. Explore alternatives to traditional canvases, such as those made from recycled or organic materials. Dive into the world of eco-friendly paints, where water-based and plant-based options offer vibrant hues without harming the environment. Green Canvas introduces you to a palette of sustainable choices that leave both your artwork and the planet feeling refreshed.

Consider experimenting with unconventional surfaces like reclaimed wood, repurposed fabrics, or even recycled paper to make your artistic endeavors not just visually appealing but also environmentally responsible.

Upcycled Wonders: Breathing Life into Discarded Objects

In "Upcycled Wonders," we celebrate the art of giving new life to old, discarded objects. Uncover the beauty in repurposing materials that would otherwise end up in landfills. From sculptures crafted from reclaimed metal to mosaics made from broken tiles, discover how upcycled art can be a powerful statement against waste.

Consider attending local flea markets or exploring thrift stores for materials that can be transformed into unique art pieces. Upcycled Wonders proves that creativity can thrive while simultaneously reducing your ecological footprint.

Nature's Palette: Botanical Art and Sustainable Inks

In "Nature's Palette," we explore the world of botanical art and sustainable inks. Dive into the realm of art made from pressed flowers, leaves, and other natural elements. Learn about inks derived from plant pigments, minimizing the use of harmful chemicals. Nature's Palette not only brings the outdoors in but also showcases how sustainable choices can enhance the beauty of your artistic expressions.

Consider creating your botanical art by pressing flowers from your garden or sourcing materials locally. Nature's Palette demonstrates that sustainable art can be a breath of fresh air in your home.

Recycled Revelations: Paper and Cardboard Art

In "Recycled Revelations," we turn our attention to paper and cardboard art. Discover how discarded newspapers, magazines, and cardboard can be transformed into stunning sculptures, collages, and installations. Dive into the world of papier-mâché, where old paper finds new purpose in the creation of unique and sustainable art.

Consider organizing paper and cardboard recycling bins in your home, encouraging the collection of materials for your artistic projects. Recycled Revelations showcases that with a bit of creativity, your trash can become your treasure.

Lighting the Way: Sustainable Illuminated Art

In "Lighting the Way," we shed light on sustainable illuminated art. Explore the world of eco-friendly lighting options for your artwork, such as energy-efficient LED bulbs and solar-powered fixtures. Discover how backlit art installations can not only enhance your living space aesthetically but also contribute to energy conservation.

Consider incorporating renewable energy sources into your home, such as solar panels, to power your illuminated art pieces. Lighting the Way illuminates the potential for sustainable choices to brighten both your home and the planet.

The Circular Canvas: Art as a Catalyst for Recycling

In "The Circular Canvas," we explore how art can be a catalyst for recycling. Learn about artists who use their creative skills to raise awareness about recycling and repurposing materials. Discover how your own art projects can inspire others to adopt a more circular approach to consumption.

Consider organizing local art events that focus on using recycled materials, fostering a sense of community engagement in sustainable practices. The Circular Canvas showcases the power of art to not only reflect but also drive positive environmental change.

Conclusion:

As we conclude our journey through "Eco-Friendly Art: Sustainable Choices for a Greener Home," let's celebrate the potential of art to make a positive impact on our planet. From green canvases to upcycled wonders, Nature's Palette to Recycled Revelations, each section demonstrates that sustainability and creativity can go hand in hand. Embrace eco-friendly art, and let your home become a gallery of inspiration for a greener, more conscious world.

CREATING FOCAL POINTS: USING WALL ART TO DIRECT ATTENTION IN SPACES

Step into the world where art takes center stage, guiding the eye and influencing the ambiance of a space. In "Creating Focal Points: Using Wall Art to Direct Attention in Spaces," we unravel the artistry behind orchestrating visual experiences that captivate and direct attention seamlessly.

THE ART OF FIRST IMPRESSIONS: CRAFTING ENTRANCES THAT COMMAND ATTENTION

In "The Art of First Impressions," discover how strategic placement of captivating art pieces at entrances sets the tone for the entire space. Explore the psychological impact of the initial visual encounter and how it shapes visitors' perceptions. Uncover techniques for curating an entrance that not only commands attention but leaves a lasting impression.

Consider the use of bold and vibrant art pieces strategically placed at entrances, creating a focal point that welcomes and captivates anyone who steps into the space.

Mastering the Art of Balance: Creating Harmonious Focal Points

In "Mastering the Art of Balance," we delve into the delicate balance of creating focal points that enhance rather than overwhelm a space. Explore the principles of design, color, and scale that contribute to the creation of harmonious visual experiences. Witness how thoughtful curation can transform a room, drawing attention to specific areas while maintaining an overall sense of balance.

Consider incorporating a mix of statement pieces and complementary artworks to create a balanced yet visually engaging atmosphere, ensuring that each focal point complements the others.

Strategic Placement: Directing Attention with Purpose

In "Strategic Placement," explore the intentional positioning of art to guide the flow of attention within a space. Delve into the psychology of human gaze and movement, understanding how art can act as visual cues, leading visitors through a carefully curated journey. Learn how strategic placement contributes to a narrative within a room, ensuring a seamless and intentional visual experience.

Consider the flow of movement within a space and
the natural path that visitors might take. Strategically place focal point artworks along this path to guide their attention and create a purposeful visual journey.

Scaling Up: Using Size to Emphasize Importance

In "Scaling Up," discover the impact of size in creating focal points that demand attention. Explore how oversized artworks can dominate a space, becoming a central focus that draws the eye. Understand the psychological effect of scale and how it can be leveraged to emphasize the importance of specific areas or features within a room.

Consider incorporating large-scale artworks in areas where you want to create a dominant focal point, making a bold statement that anchors the visual experience in that particular space.

Contrast and Bold Choices: Making Focal Points Unforgettable

In "Contrast and Bold Choices," we explore the use of contrast and daring choices in creating unforgettable focal points. Dive into the world of unexpected color palettes, unconventional materials, and striking designs that demand attention. Witness how the element of surprise can elevate a focal point, leaving a lasting impression on those who engage with the space.

Consider experimenting with bold and contrasting choices in your focal point artworks, ensuring that they stand out and contribute to the overall uniqueness of the space.

Evolving Focal Points: Seasonal and Rotating Art Displays

In "Evolving Focal Points," we conclude our exploration by considering the dynamic aspect of focal points. Explore the concept of seasonal and rotating art displays that inject freshness into a space. Learn how the evolution of focal points can keep a space dynamic, inviting visitors to return and discover new points of interest.

Consider incorporating a rotation of artworks or seasonal displays to keep the focal points in your space ever-changing, providing a sense of novelty and excitement for returning visitors.

In Conclusion:

In the tapestry of "Creating Focal Points: Using Wall Art to Direct Attention in Spaces," we've unraveled the artful strategies behind orchestrating visual experiences that command attention and shape the overall ambiance of a space. From crafting impactful entrances and mastering the art of balance to strategic placement, scaling up, bold choices, and evolving focal points, the journey of guiding attention through art is a dynamic and ever-evolving one. As we navigate these creative realms, we empower spaces to become immersive narratives, each one telling a unique and compelling story.

WALL WONDERS: THE TRANSFORMATIVE MAGIC OF STATEMENT PIECES IN LARGE WALL ART

Step into a realm where your walls become not just canvases but portals to a world of visual delight. In this blog post, we'll unravel the enchanting power of statement pieces – large wall art that transcends mere decoration, transforming your space into a gallery of unparalleled elegance. From the bold strokes of color to the intricate details that command attention, join us on a journey of discovering the transformative magic that large wall art brings to the heart of your home.

Larger Than Life: The Allure of Large Wall Art Statement Pieces:

If your walls could speak, they would shout with the grandeur of large wall art statement pieces. These commanding artworks are not just decorative elements; they are declarations of style and personality. The allure lies in their ability to dominate a space, making a bold and confident statement that captures the attention of anyone who enters the room.

Consider a sprawling canvas that engulfs your living room wall or an oversized framed print that acts as the focal point of your dining area. Large wall art is not just about size; it's about making an impact. The visual weight and presence of these pieces elevate the ambiance of a room, turning it into a curated sanctuary where art takes center stage.

Transforming Spaces with Statement Wall Art:

The transformative power of statement wall art goes beyond mere aesthetics; it reshapes the very essence of a space. A well-chosen piece has the ability to dictate the mood and theme of a room, turning a blank canvas into a narrative of color, emotion, and style. Whether you opt for a vibrant abstract masterpiece or a captivating photograph that tells a story, the transformative journey begins the moment the art meets the wall.

Large wall art has the unique ability to tie together disparate elements in a room, creating a cohesive and harmonious atmosphere. It can complement existing decor or become the catalyst for a complete style overhaul. By transforming spaces with statement wall art, you infuse personality into your home, making it an extension of your unique taste and creative expression.

The Powerhouse Impact: Large Art's Powerful Influence on Home Decor:

The impact of large wall art on home decor is akin to a powerhouse of influence. It's not just about filling a void; it's about curating an experience. These statement pieces set the tone for the entire room, creating a visual rhythm that resonates with the occupants. The choice of artwork can evoke emotions, stimulate conversation, or even transport you to a different time and place.

Consider the power of a large abstract painting in a minimalist space, adding a burst of energy and personality. Alternatively, a photographic mural capturing the essence of nature can bring a sense of tranquility to your bedroom. The impact is not limited to the visual; it extends to how you feel within the space. Large wall art becomes a dynamic force, influencing the ambiance and leaving an indelible mark on your home decor.

Beyond Traditional Boundaries: Unleashing Creativity with Large Wall Art:

One of the most exciting aspects of large wall art statement pieces is the freedom they offer to unleash creativity beyond traditional boundaries. These pieces challenge the conventions of art display, encouraging experimentation with scale, composition, and placement. Consider a triptych that spans across multiple walls or an art installation that defies the confines of a single frame.

Large wall art provides an opportunity to think outside the box, allowing you to curate a space that is truly unique. Embrace the unconventional – mix and match different styles, play with asymmetry, or even combine various mediums to create a visually arresting collage. Beyond traditional boundaries, large wall art becomes a canvas for your creativity, turning your home into a living art installation.

Making a Statement in Every Room: Tailoring Large Art to Spaces:

The beauty of large wall art lies in its versatility – it can make a statement in every room of your home. From the living room to the bedroom, the kitchen to the hallway, these pieces have the power to tailor the ambiance to suit the function and personality of each space. Consider tailoring large art to spaces, selecting pieces that resonate with the purpose and energy of each room.

In the living room, opt for a bold and vibrant piece that sparks conversation and exudes warmth. In the bedroom, choose art that promotes relaxation and serenity, perhaps a soothing landscape or an abstract piece with calming hues. The kitchen can be adorned with lively and energetic art, adding a touch of dynamism to the heart of your home. By making a statement in every room, large wall art ensures that each space is a curated masterpiece.

The Curator's Touch: How to Choose and Showcase Large Wall Art:

Choosing and showcasing large wall art is an art form in itself, requiring the curator's touch to bring out the full potential of these statement pieces. Consider the overall theme and color scheme of the room – does the art complement or contrast? Pay attention to the size and scale; large wall art should fill the space without overwhelming it.

Experiment with different hanging styles – a single, oversized piece as a focal point, a gallery wall for a curated look, or even leaning art against the wall for a laid-back, casual vibe. The key is to strike a balance between the art and the room's architecture. The curator's touch involves a keen eye for aesthetics, an understanding of the room's purpose, and the ability to let the art breathe and command attention in its own unique way.

Conclusion:

As we conclude our journey into the world of large wall art statement pieces, remember that the magic lies in the ability to transform your space into a visual masterpiece. These commanding artworks go beyond mere decoration; they are expressions of style, statements of personality, and catalysts for a transformative experience. Whether you opt for the bold strokes of abstract art or the captivating narratives of photography, large wall art has the power to turn your home into a gallery where every wall is a canvas waiting to be adorned.

BRUSHING LIFE ONTO YOUR WALLS: THE MAGIC OF PERSONALIZED WALL ART

Step into a world where your walls tell a story, where every brushstroke transforms a blank canvas into a personalized masterpiece. In this blog post, we'll delve into the transformative power of wall art and how it has the magic to turn a house into a home. From home decor wall art ideas to the enchanting realm of personalized creations, let's explore the journey of infusing your living space with a touch that is uniquely yours.

1. Unveiling the Magic of Wall Art:

Your walls are more than just boundaries; they are the blank pages of your life's story. Wall art, with its mesmerizing allure, has the power to unveil the magic within these spaces. It's not just about filling an empty void; it's about creating an atmosphere, setting a mood, and expressing your personality. The simple act of adorning your walls with carefully curated pieces can transform a room from mere functionality to a sanctuary of emotions and memories.

Transitioning from generic wall decor to art that resonates with you is a journey into self-expression. Consider investing in pieces that evoke emotions, whether it's a vibrant abstract painting or a serene landscape. The magic lies in finding art that speaks to you, that tells your story in a language only you can understand. As you embark on this journey, let your walls become the canvas where your life's narrative unfolds.

2. Home Decor Wall Art Ideas:

The world of home decor wall art ideas is an expansive playground waiting for your creative exploration. Gone are the days of traditional framed prints; today, it's about breaking free from the ordinary. Create a gallery wall that weaves together a tapestry of memories – family photos, travel snapshots, and art that resonates with your soul. Experiment with shapes, sizes, and textures to add depth and visual interest to your space. The goal is to turn your walls into a curated gallery that reflects not just your style but the essence of who you are.

Consider incorporating unconventional materials into your wall decor, like metal or reclaimed wood, to add a touch of uniqueness. Mix and match different styles – vintage with contemporary, minimalistic with bold – for an eclectic and personalized look. Home decor wall art ideas are limited only by your imagination, so let it run wild as you transform your living space into a gallery of self-expression.

3. Personalized Wall Art for Home:

If walls could speak, what would yours say? Personalized wall art is the answer to infusing your home with a unique touch that resonates with your personality. This goes beyond choosing generic prints; it's about creating custom pieces that tell your story. Consider a canvas adorned with your favorite quote, a family tree mural in the hallway, or a collage of memories capturing the essence of your life's journey. Personalized wall art turns your living space into a canvas of memories, a testament to the beauty of individuality.

The beauty of personalized wall art is its ability to make your home truly yours. It's a constant reminder of what you love, where you've been, and the dreams you're chasing. Collaborate with artists or embark on DIY projects to create pieces that hold sentimental value. As you adorn your walls with personalized creations, you're not just decorating; you're writing the chapters of your life in strokes of color and creativity.

4. The Power of Colors:

Colors are the silent storytellers in the tapestry of wall art. They have the power to evoke emotions, set the tone, and create a harmonious atmosphere. When transforming your home with wall art, consider the palette you're introducing. Vibrant colors can inject energy into a room, while muted tones create a sense of calm. Pay attention to the existing color scheme in your space, ensuring that the artwork complements and enhances the overall ambiance.

Experiment with the psychology of colors – use blues and greens for a tranquil bedroom, reds and yellows for an energetic kitchen, or earthy tones for a cozy living room. The power of colors is not just visual; it's emotional. Let your walls be a canvas where the colors dance in harmony, creating an environment that resonates with your desired mood and energy.

5. Creating a Focal Point:

Every room needs a focal point, a visual anchor that captures attention and sets the tone. Wall art serves as the perfect tool to create these captivating focal points. Whether it's an oversized canvas above the fireplace, a striking sculpture in the entryway, or a carefully curated gallery wall, the focal point becomes the heartbeat of the room. It's the element that ties everything together and invites admiration.

Consider the architecture and layout of each room when selecting or creating a focal point. It could be a piece that contrasts with the overall theme, adding a touch of drama, or one that seamlessly blends into the existing decor, providing a subtle yet powerful anchor. By creating focal points with wall art, you guide the eyes, tell a visual story, and elevate the aesthetics of your home to new heights.

6. Artistic Arrangements:

The art of arranging your wall art is a skill that can turn a collection of pieces into a cohesive and visually appealing display. Experiment with different layouts to find what suits your style and the room's dimensions. Symmetry lends a sense of order and balance, while asymmetry brings a dynamic and casual vibe. Play with spacing, heights, and orientations to create a composition that engages the eye.

Consider the flow between pieces – whether it's a series of framed prints, a gallery wall, or a mix of sculptures and paintings. The arrangement should feel intentional, allowing the viewer's eyes to travel seamlessly across the display. Artistic arrangements not only enhance the aesthetic appeal of your home but also showcase your thoughtfulness in curating a space that tells a story.

Conclusion:

As we conclude our exploration into the magic of personalized wall art, remember that transforming your home is not just about filling spaces but about creating an environment that resonates with your essence. From home decor wall art ideas that spark your creativity to personalized creations that tell your story, every piece contributes to the symphony of your living space. Let your walls become the canvas where your life's narrative unfolds, where colors dance, and where memories find a permanent place. In the realm of wall art, you hold the brush, and your home is the masterpiece.

RADIANCE AND CANVAS: ILLUMINATING YOUR SPACE WITH ART AND LIGHTING HARMONY

Step into a world where art and lighting converge to create a symphony of radiance and ambiance. In this blog post, we'll explore the transformative power of combining art and lighting, turning your living space into a captivating gallery of illuminated masterpieces. From strategic spotlighting to integrated LED art, join us on a journey through the harmonious relationship between art and lighting, where each piece becomes a radiant focal point, enhancing the overall ambiance of your home.

1. Spotlight on Mastery: The Art of Strategic Lighting:

Our first spotlight is on the mastery of strategic lighting, where thoughtful placement of spotlights and accent lights enhances the beauty of individual artworks. Consider strategically positioning adjustable spotlights above or below your favorite pieces to create a dramatic play of light and shadow. This technique not only draws attention to the artwork but also adds depth and dimension to the surrounding space.

Experiment with different angles and intensities to find the perfect balance that highlights the textures and details of the artwork. The art of strategic lighting extends beyond paintings to sculptures, wall installations, and even decorative elements. Let your walls come alive with the mastery of strategic lighting, transforming your art collection into a gallery that dazzles with radiant allure.

2. Luminous Canvases: Integrating LED Art for a Modern Glow:

Embark on a journey into the world of luminous canvases, where integrating LED art brings a modern glow to your space. LED-lit artworks combine the beauty of visual art with the functionality of ambient lighting, creating pieces that are both decorative and illuminating. From backlit canvases to sculptures with embedded LEDs, this contemporary approach to art and lighting adds a touch of futuristic elegance to your home.

Consider selecting LED art pieces that complement your overall decor style, whether it's a minimalist design with clean lines or a bold statement with vibrant colors. The luminous canvases not only serve as captivating art installations but also contribute to the overall ambiance of your room. Embrace the synergy of art and LED lighting, and let your walls become radiant focal points that redefine modern sophistication.

3. Shadow Play: Intriguing Forms with Artful Shadows:

Delve into the enchanting world of shadow play, where strategic lighting creates intriguing forms and artful shadows. By positioning lights at varying distances and angles, you can cast captivating shadows that add an extra layer of visual interest to your art collection. This technique works exceptionally well with sculptures, wall reliefs, and three-dimensional art pieces.

Experiment with different types of lighting, such as wall-mounted sconces or pendant lights, to cast shadows that interact dynamically with the artwork. The interplay of light and shadow adds a touch of mystery and depth, turning your walls into a canvas for ever-changing visual experiences. Embrace the artful dance of shadow play, and watch as your space becomes a captivating theater of light and form.

4. Ambient Elegance: Overhead Lighting for Overall Atmosphere:

Illuminate your space with ambient elegance, where overhead lighting contributes to the overall atmosphere of your room. While strategic spotlights draw attention to specific artworks, ambient lighting sets the mood for the entire space. Consider pendant lights, chandeliers, or even recessed lighting to provide a warm and inviting glow that bathes your art collection and surrounding decor in a harmonious ambiance.

Choose fixtures that complement the style of your artworks and enhance the overall aesthetic of your space. The goal is to create a balanced and well-lit environment that showcases your art while ensuring a comfortable and welcoming atmosphere. Ambient elegance transforms your home into a sanctuary of art and light, inviting you to relax and bask in the radiant glow of artistic ambiance.

5. Functional Illumination: Art as Task Lighting in Everyday Spaces:

Explore the concept of functional illumination, where art serves a dual purpose as task lighting in everyday spaces. This approach involves integrating artworks with lighting elements into functional areas such as home offices, reading nooks, or kitchen spaces. Picture wall-mounted art fixtures with adjustable reading lights or sculptures that double as desk lamps.

Consider selecting art pieces that not only complement the aesthetic of the room but also fulfill a practical purpose. Functional illumination seamlessly merges artistry with utility, ensuring that your living spaces are both visually pleasing and highly functional. Embrace the marriage of form and function with art as task lighting, and let your everyday spaces become illuminated canvases of both beauty and practicality.

6. Outdoor Radiance: Extending Art and Lighting to Outdoor Spaces:

Conclude our exploration by stepping into the realm of outdoor radiance, where the fusion of art and lighting extends beyond the confines of your home. Illuminate your outdoor spaces with strategically placed lights that highlight sculptures, garden installations, or even outdoor artwork. Whether it's a well-lit pathway or a sculptural centerpiece, outdoor radiance transforms your exterior spaces into an extension of your artistic expression.

Consider weather-resistant fixtures, solar-powered lights, or integrated LEDs in outdoor artworks to create a captivating nighttime display. The interplay of light and art in outdoor settings enhances curb appeal and provides an inviting atmosphere for evening gatherings. Embrace the enchantment of outdoor radiance, and let your art and lighting extend the beauty of your home into the open air.

In Conclusion:

As we conclude our journey through the interplay of art and lighting, remember that the magic lies in the seamless integration of these two elements to create a harmonious and

 captivating living space. Whether you choose the mastery of strategic lighting, luminous canvases with integrated LEDs, shadow play for intriguing forms, ambient elegance with overhead lighting, functional illumination in everyday spaces, or outdoor radiance that extends the magic beyond your walls, let your home become a radiant canvas where art and lighting dance in perfect harmony.

HARMONY IN HUES: MASTERING ARTISTIC ARRANGEMENTS FOR A VISUAL SYMPHONY ON YOUR WALLS

Embark on a journey of visual delight as we explore the art of creating harmony on your walls through artistic arrangements. In this blog post, we'll unravel the secrets of arranging artworks in a way that transforms your space into a captivating visual symphony. From gallery walls to thematic displays, join us in discovering the creative possibilities that go beyond mere decoration, turning your walls into a curated masterpiece that reflects your unique style and personality.

The Gallery Wall Extravaganza: Crafting a Visual Tapestry of Personal Treasures:

Our first destination is the gallery wall extravaganza, where an eclectic mix of artworks converges to create a visual tapestry of personal treasures. This arrangement style allows you to showcase a diverse collection of art pieces, including paintings, prints, photographs, and even 3D objects. The key to mastering the gallery wall is to strike a balance between cohesion and individuality.

Consider arranging artworks in a grid for a clean and organized look, or opt for a more organic and asymmetrical layout for a dynamic and eclectic feel. The gallery wall extravaganza is an excellent opportunity to blend different styles, sizes, and frame colors, creating a curated display that tells a visual story about your life and interests. Let your walls become a canvas for self-expression with a gallery wall extravaganza that transforms your space into an art lover's haven.

Thematic Marvels: Curating Walls with a Unified Aesthetic:

Venture into the world of thematic marvels, where walls become a curated canvas with a unified aesthetic. Thematic arrangements involve selecting artworks that share a common theme, whether it's a specific color palette, subject matter, or artistic style. This approach allows you to create a cohesive and intentional look that ties your space together.

Consider exploring themes such as nature-inspired art, abstract expressions, or even a specific art movement. Thematic marvels provide a curated visual experience, turning your walls into a gallery with a deliberate narrative. This arrangement style is particularly effective in spaces where a specific atmosphere or mood is desired. Embrace the power of thematic marvels and watch as your walls become a curated masterpiece that reflects your aesthetic sensibilities.

Symmetry and Simplicity: Creating Visual Calm with Balanced Arrangements:

Step into the realm of symmetry and simplicity, where balanced arrangements create a visual calm that brings a sense of order to your walls. This approach involves arranging artworks in a symmetrical fashion, either by mirroring the placement of identical pieces or creating a harmonious balance with different but visually similar items.

Consider opting for identical frames and matting for a clean and cohesive look or choose artworks with similar sizes and visual weight to maintain balance. Symmetry and simplicity are ideal for spaces where a sense of tranquility and order is desired, such as bedrooms or home offices. Let your walls become a source of visual calm with balanced arrangements that showcase the beauty of simplicity.

The Eclectic Ensemble: Mixing and Matching for Visual Dynamism:

Embark on a journey into the eclectic ensemble, where mixing and matching different art styles, periods, and mediums create visual dynamism and a sense of intrigue. This arrangement style is perfect for those who appreciate an eclectic and layered aesthetic, allowing you to showcase your diverse tastes and artistic preferences.

Consider combining contemporary pieces with vintage finds, abstract expressions with figurative artworks, and even diverse framing styles for added interest. The eclectic ensemble thrives on the unexpected, turning your walls into a gallery of delightful surprises. This arrangement style is particularly effective in open and communal spaces where visual diversity can be fully appreciated. Embrace the excitement of the eclectic ensemble and watch as your walls become a celebration of artistic diversity.

The Vertical Ascension: Elevating Style with Floor-to-Ceiling Arrangements:

Ascend to new heights with the vertical ascension, where floor-to-ceiling arrangements make a bold and stylish statement. This arrangement style involves maximizing the vertical space on your walls, creating a visually striking display that draws the eye upward. From large-scale artworks to vertically stacked frames, the vertical ascension adds a touch of grandeur and sophistication to your space.

Consider incorporating a mix of different-sized artworks or arranging a series of vertically aligned pieces for a cohesive look. The vertical ascension is particularly effective in rooms with high ceilings, creating a sense of verticality and elegance. Let your walls become a canvas for upward style with floor-to-ceiling arrangements that elevate the visual impact of your living space.

Personalized Collages: Crafting Intimate Displays with Personal Touches:

Conclude our exploration with personalized collages, where intimate displays and personal touches turn your walls into a reflection of cherished memories and meaningful objects. This arrangement style involves combining artworks with personal items such as photographs, letters, or even three-dimensional objects that hold sentimental value.

Consider crafting a collage that tells a story about your life, incorporating elements that evoke nostalgia and personal connection. Personalized collages are ideal for spaces where an intimate and welcoming atmosphere is desired, such as family rooms or home offices. Embrace the sentimentality of personalized collages and watch as your walls become a heartfelt display that resonates with warmth and personal significance.

Conclusion:

As we conclude our journey through the world of artistic arrangements, remember that the key lies in infusing your unique personality and style into the curation of your walls. Whether you're drawn to the gallery wall extravaganza, thematic marvels, symmetry and simplicity, the eclectic ensemble, the vertical ascension, or personalized collages, let your walls become a canvas for self-expression and creativity. Transform your living space into a visual symphony that resonates with your individuality and adds a touch of artistry to every corner.

TIMELESS TREASURES: BLENDING ERAS WITH ANTIQUE WALL ART IN CONTEMPORARY SPACES

Step into the world where vintage meets modern, where the charm of the past seamlessly blends with the aesthetics of today. In this blog post, we'll explore the art of incorporating antique wall art in modern homes, adding character, history, and a touch of nostalgia to contemporary spaces. Join us on a journey of discovering timeless treasures that bridge the gap between eras, creating a unique and inviting atmosphere in your living space.

Navigating Time Travel: The Allure of Antique Wall Art:

Embark on a journey of time travel as we explore the allure of antique wall art. Vintage pieces bring a sense of history, craftsmanship, and nostalgia that can't be replicated with contemporary artworks. Whether it's a weathered map, an ornate mirror, or a faded botanical print, antique wall art tells a story and serves as a visual reminder of eras gone by. The allure lies not just in the aesthetic appeal but in the emotional connection that these pieces evoke.

Consider exploring local antique shops, flea markets, or even family heirlooms to discover unique treasures. The charm of antique wall art lies in its ability to add depth and personality to modern homes, creating a conversation between the past and the present. Navigating time travel through antique wall art allows you to curate a space that reflects your appreciation for history and design.

Classic Elegance: Elevating Modern Spaces with Vintage Frames:

Incorporate classic elegance into modern spaces by embracing vintage frames for your wall art. Antique frames, with their intricate details, gilded finishes, or distressed patinas, add a touch of timeless sophistication to any artwork. Whether you choose to showcase family photographs, vintage postcards, or contemporary prints within these frames, the juxtaposition creates a harmonious blend of classic and modern aesthetics.

Experiment with a mix of frame styles and sizes to create a gallery wall that exudes classic elegance. The ornate details of antique frames draw attention to the artwork while seamlessly integrating with the overall design of a room. Elevating modern spaces with vintage frames allows you to curate a visual narrative that is both sophisticated and rooted in the enduring beauty of the past.

Patina Magic: Embracing the Worn and Weathered Look:

Unlock the magic of patina as we delve into the art of embracing the worn and weathered look in antique wall art. Patina adds character, authenticity, and a sense of lived-in charm to vintage pieces. Whether it's a distressed painting, a rusted metal sign, or a faded tapestry, the imperfections tell a tale of time and create a unique focal point within a modern interior.

To embrace the patina magic, allow yourself to appreciate the beauty of aged materials. Don't be afraid of scratches, faded colors, or chipped paint; these elements contribute to the vintage appeal. The worn and weathered look in antique wall art transforms your home into a haven of stories, each mark representing a chapter in the life of the piece and adding a layer of intrigue to your space.

Eclectic Pairings: Modern Art Meets Vintage Charm:

Break the mold of traditional design by exploring eclectic pairings where modern art meets vintage charm. In this section, we'll explore the delightful juxtaposition of contemporary artworks alongside antique pieces. Consider placing a sleek abstract painting next to a vintage mirror or hanging a gallery of modern prints above an antique sideboard.

The beauty of eclectic pairings lies in the unexpected harmony created between disparate elements. Modern art and antique wall pieces engage in a visual dialogue that adds energy and interest to your space. Embrace the freedom to experiment with combinations that resonate with your style, allowing your home to become a canvas where different eras coexist in a delightful dance of design.

Whimsical Time Capsules: Incorporating Antique Curiosities:

Transform your home into whimsical time capsules by incorporating antique curiosities as wall art. Vintage maps, clocks, keys, or even industrial artifacts can become intriguing focal points that transport your space to another era. Create a thematic wall arrangement that showcases a collection of antique curiosities, turning your walls into a gallery of time-traveling wonders.

Consider the stories behind each piece – the journeys of old keys, the history embodied in vintage maps, or the mechanical beauty of an antique clock. These curiosities not only serve as wall art but also as conversation starters, inviting guests to step into a world where the past mingles with the present. The incorporation of antique curiosities adds a touch of whimsy and narrative depth to modern homes.

DIY Vintage: Crafting Timeless Art with a Modern Twist:

Conclude our exploration by embracing the DIY spirit and crafting timeless art with a modern twist. Combine your love for vintage aesthetics with a contemporary touch by creating your own antique-inspired wall art. Consider distressing a mirror frame, repurposing old photographs into a collage, or using antique botanical illustrations as inspiration for hand-painted canvases.

DIY vintage projects allow you to infuse your personal style into the antique aesthetic, creating pieces that are uniquely yours. Whether you're a seasoned crafter or a beginner, the process of crafting vintage-inspired art adds a layer of authenticity and personal connection to your home. Elevate the DIY vintage spirit by showcasing your creations alongside genuine antique pieces, creating a dynamic blend of old and new.

Conclusion:

As we conclude our journey through the world of timeless treasures and the art of incorporating antique wall art in modern homes, remember that the magic lies in the balance between eras. Vintage pieces have the remarkable ability to add warmth, depth, and character to contemporary spaces, creating a home that reflects not just your style, but the stories of the past. So, go ahead, embrace the allure of antique wall art, and let your living space become a canvas where time intertwines in a symphony of design.

ART IN UNEXPECTED PLACES: HALLWAYS AND CORRIDORS EDITION

Welcome to a creative exploration of "Art in Unexpected Places: Hallways and Corridors Edition." Often overlooked, these transitional spaces offer a unique canvas for artistic expression. In this blog post, we'll guide you through innovative ideas and inspiring examples, proving that art can transform the mundane into the extraordinary. Join us as we turn these neglected passageways into vibrant galleries that tell stories, evoke emotions, and captivate anyone who walks through.

The Gallery Entry: Setting the Tone

In "The Gallery Entry," discover how to make a bold statement from the moment someone steps into your home. Hallways serve as the prelude to your living space, making them the perfect place to introduce your artistic theme. Whether it's a series of framed photographs, a curated collection of small sculptures, or an oversized abstract painting, the gallery entry sets the tone for the visual journey ahead.

Consider selecting pieces that resonate with the overall aesthetic of your home, providing a sneak peek into the artistic narrative that unfolds within. The Gallery Entry transforms your hallway into a captivating introduction, sparking curiosity and inviting exploration.

Mural Magic: Transforming Long Corridors

In "Mural Magic," we explore the transformative power of murals in long corridors. Murals offer a seamless way to infuse color, depth, and narrative into an otherwise monotonous space. From nature-inspired scenes to abstract expressions, these large-scale artworks can visually elongate and enhance the architectural features of your hallway.

Consider collaborating with a local artist to create a custom mural that complements the flow and dimensions of your corridor. Mural Magic encourages you to think beyond traditional wall decor and embrace the immersive experience of a hallway mural.

Framed Narratives: Creating a Storyline

In "Framed Narratives," we delve into the concept of creating a storyline within your hallway using framed art. Explore the art of storytelling by curating a collection of artworks that together convey a cohesive narrative. This could be a chronological series of family photos, a progression of abstract pieces, or even a thematic arrangement that tells a visual tale.

Consider incorporating small plaques or captions beneath each frame, providing context and enhancing the narrative flow. Framed Narratives turns your hallway into a dynamic storyboard, engaging both the eyes and the imagination of those who traverse through.

Light and Shadow: Sculpting with Sconces

In "Light and Shadow," discover the sculptural potential of incorporating wall sconces along your hallway. Art isn't limited to what hangs on the walls; it can also be the play of light and shadow. Strategically placing sconces with unique designs creates an interplay of shadows that adds a dynamic, three-dimensional element to your corridor.

Consider selecting sconces with intricate patterns or sculptural shapes, turning your hallway into a mesmerizing interplay of light and shadow. Light and Shadow introduces a new dimension to your art exploration, showcasing that art can be an ever-changing spectacle.

Interactive Installations: Engaging the Senses

In "Interactive Installations," we explore the concept of engaging the senses through art. Transform your hallway into an interactive space with installations that invite touch, sound, or even scent. From textured wall panels to wind chimes or fragrant wall diffusers, these elements add a multisensory dimension to your corridor.

Consider incorporating small seating areas or benches along the hallway, encouraging visitors to pause, interact, and fully immerse themselves in the artistic experience. Interactive Installations challenge the conventional notion of passive observation, turning your hallway into an evolving and engaging space.

Underfoot Artistry: Statement Runners and Rugs

In "Underfoot Artistry," we shift our focus downward to explore how statement runners and rugs can become art pieces in their own right. Elevate your corridor by selecting bold patterns, vibrant colors, or unique textures for your floor coverings. This unconventional approach transforms the often-neglected floor into a canvas for artistic expression.

Consider opting for a custom-designed runner that complements the overall aesthetic of your home or selecting a rug with an abstract pattern that serves as a conversation starter. Underfoot Artistry challenges the traditional notion of wall-centric art, proving that creativity can extend to every corner of your hallway.

Conclusion:

As we conclude our journey through "Art in Unexpected Places: Hallways and Corridors Edition," take a moment to reconsider the untapped potential of these transitional spaces. From the gallery entry to underfoot artistry, each section has illuminated the myriad ways you can infuse creativity into hallways and corridors. By embracing the unexpected, you can turn these passageways into dynamic canvases that leave a lasting impression on anyone who walks through.

BLOSSOMING WALLS: EMBRACING NATURE WITH BOTANICAL BEAUTY IN WALL ART

Step into a world of natural elegance as we explore the enchanting realm of botanical beauty in wall art. In this blog post, we'll dive into the ways you can infuse your living space with the freshness and vibrancy of plant-themed wall art. From lush landscapes to detailed illustrations, join us on a journey of embracing nature within your home and transforming your walls into blooming canvases that celebrate the beauty of the botanical world.

THE GREEN REVOLUTION: TRANSFORMING WALLS WITH LARGE BOTANICAL MURALS:

Our first stop on this botanical journey is the green revolution, where we explore the transformative power of large botanical murals. Imagine walls adorned with oversized, life-like depictions of your favorite plants – from towering palms to intricate ferns. Large botanical murals create a visual impact, turning ordinary walls into immersive landscapes that bring the outdoors in.

Consider choosing a mural that complements the overall theme of your room, whether it's a tropical paradise for a relaxed vibe or a forest scene for a touch of tranquility. The beauty of large botanical murals lies in their ability to redefine the entire atmosphere of a space, making it feel like a natural oasis. Let the green revolution breathe life into your home, and watch as walls burst into bloom with the grandeur of botanical beauty.

Floral Fantasia: Infusing Romance with Flower-themed Wall Art:

Venture into the realm of floral fantasia, where walls come alive with the romance and delicacy of flower-themed wall art. Picture an array of floral prints, canvas paintings, or even floral decals that infuse your space with the timeless beauty of blossoms. From vibrant roses to delicate cherry blossoms, floral-themed wall art adds a touch of romance and grace to any room.

Consider creating a focal point with a statement piece, such as a large canvas featuring a single bold flower, or opt for a gallery wall that showcases the diversity of floral beauty. The versatility of floral fantasia allows you to experiment with different color palettes, styles, and flower varieties, ensuring that your space reflects your unique aesthetic. Infuse your home with the enchanting allure of flowers, turning walls into a canvas of perpetual spring.

Tropical Retreat: Evoking Paradise with Exotic Plant Wall Art:

Escape to a tropical retreat within the confines of your home as we explore the allure of exotic plant wall art. Envision walls adorned with palm trees, monstera leaves, and vibrant tropical blooms that evoke the paradise of a distant island. Tropical-themed wall art brings a sense of relaxation and sophistication, transforming your space into a haven of warmth and exotic charm.

Consider incorporating botanical prints with a mix of bold and subtle colors to capture the vibrancy of a tropical paradise. Whether you choose a single statement piece or a collage of tropical delights, let the allure of exotic plant wall art transport you to the serenity of a sun-drenched getaway. Turn your home into a tropical retreat where the beauty of nature becomes a part of your everyday living.

Minimalist Greenery: Embracing Simplicity with Subtle Plant Silhouettes:

Enter the world of minimalist greenery, where subtlety meets sophistication with plant silhouettes adorning your walls. Minimalist plant-themed wall art embraces simplicity, featuring elegant outlines of leaves, branches, or potted plants. The understated beauty of these silhouettes adds a touch of modernity and tranquility to your space.

Consider arranging a series of framed plant silhouettes in a symmetrical or asymmetrical pattern to create visual interest. The neutral tones and clean lines of minimalist greenery make it an ideal choice for various decor styles, from contemporary to Scandinavian. Embrace the art of less-is-more with plant silhouettes that bring a sense of calm and balance to your walls, turning them into a canvas of understated elegance.

Botanical Illustrations: Elevating Walls with Detailed Plant Drawings:

Elevate your walls with the intricate beauty of botanical illustrations, where detailed plant drawings become works of art. Picture walls adorned with hand-drawn depictions of flowers, leaves, and botanical specimens that showcase the precision and artistry of nature. Botanical illustrations add a touch of sophistication and intellectual charm to your space.

Consider framing individual botanical illustrations or creating a gallery wall that celebrates the diversity of plant life. The detailed drawings allow you to appreciate the intricacies of each plant, turning your home into a botanical haven for art connoisseurs and nature enthusiasts alike. Let walls become a museum of botanical wonders with illustrations that capture the essence and beauty of the plant kingdom.

DIY Plant Art Projects: Crafting Personalized Green Masterpieces:

Conclude our exploration by delving into the world of DIY plant art projects, where you become the artist creating personalized green masterpieces for your walls. Experiment with botanical-themed crafts such as pressed flower art, leaf-printing, or even creating a botanical-inspired wall hanging. DIY plant art projects allow you to infuse your space with a touch of your own creativity and personality.

Consider involving friends or family in crafting sessions to make it a collaborative and enjoyable experience. Personalized DIY plant art adds a unique and sentimental touch to your home, turning walls into a showcase of your artistic endeavors. Let your creativity bloom with DIY plant art projects, and watch as your walls become a reflection of your passion for nature and crafting.

Conclusion:

As we conclude our journey through the world of botanical beauty in wall art, remember that the essence of nature can be seamlessly woven into the fabric of your living space. Whether you choose the green revolution of large botanical murals, the romantic allure of floral fantasia, the exotic charm of tropical retreats, the simplicity of minimalist greenery, the sophistication of botanical illustrations, or the personal touch of DIY plant art projects, let your walls become a celebration of the natural world. Infuse your home with the timeless beauty of botanicals, turning walls into a blooming sanctuary.

ART FOR ALL: THE RISE OF AFFORDABLE ELEGANCE WITH PRINT ON DEMAND

Welcome to a world where the walls of your home can be adorned with elegance without breaking the bank. In this blog post, we'll unravel the magic of print on demand art – a revolutionary concept that has made high-quality, sophisticated art accessible to everyone. From the affordability that doesn't compromise on quality to the vast array of artistic choices, join us on a journey into the realm of affordable elegance that print on demand brings to the art-loving community.

AFFORDABLE ELEGANCE IN PRINT ON DEMAND ART:

Gone are the days when the words "affordable" and "elegant" were mutually exclusive in the world of art. Print on demand has emerged as a game-changer, making high-quality art accessible to all. This innovative approach allows artists to offer their creations in a cost-effective way, bringing the beauty of elegant artwork within reach for individuals who appreciate the finer things in life but may not have a millionaire's budget.

The affordability of print on demand art doesn't mean compromising on quality. With advancements in printing technology, artists can now reproduce their work with stunning precision and detail. From canvas prints that mimic the texture of an original painting to high-quality paper prints that capture the nuance of fine details, print on demand ensures that every art lover can adorn their space with pieces that exude elegance without the hefty price tag.

The Artistic Revolution: High-Quality Art Accessible through Print on Demand:

Print on demand has sparked an artistic revolution, democratizing the world of high-quality art. Traditional art acquisition often involves hefty investments, exclusive galleries, and limited choices. However, with print on demand, the art world opens its doors wide. Talented artists from around the globe can showcase their work without the constraints of traditional art markets, and art enthusiasts can explore a vast array of styles and themes from the comfort of their homes.

This revolution is not just about accessibility; it's about diversity. Print on demand platforms feature an eclectic mix of artistic expressions – from classic paintings and contemporary illustrations to abstract wonders and niche genres. The democratization of art means that everyone can find something that resonates with their taste, allowing them to curate a personal art collection that reflects their individuality.

Print on Demand Making Art Affordable and Elegant:

The marriage of affordability and elegance in print on demand art is a testament to the evolving landscape of the art market. Artists no longer need to compromise their vision to cater to a specific demographic; instead, they can create with authenticity while making their art accessible to a broader audience. The result is a win-win scenario where both artists and art enthusiasts benefit from a symbiotic relationship.

Print on demand platforms operate on a model that prioritizes efficiency. By eliminating the need for bulk production and excessive inventory, costs are reduced, allowing artists to price their work more affordably. This affordability doesn't translate to a compromise in quality; rather, it signifies a shift in the paradigm, where elegance is no longer reserved for the elite but is a privilege extended to all who appreciate the beauty of art.

The Canvas of Choice: Exploring Artistic Diversity in Print on Demand:

One of the unique strengths of print on demand lies in its ability to cater to diverse artistic tastes. Whether you're a fan of bold and vibrant colors, minimalist designs, or intricate details, print on demand platforms offer a canvas of choice that caters to every preference. The vast range of options ensures that your walls can reflect your personality, allowing you to curate a space that feels uniquely yours.

Print on demand allows you to explore different mediums, styles, and artistic interpretations. From canvas prints that add texture to your space to framed prints that exude a polished elegance, the choices are as diverse as the artists contributing to these platforms. It's an invitation to step into a world of artistic diversity, where your walls can become a reflection of your eclectic taste and appreciation for the beauty that art brings to your life.

Beyond the Frame: Personalized Touches and Customization:

Print on demand not only brings affordability and elegance but also adds a layer of personalization to the art-buying experience. Many platforms allow you to customize your chosen artwork – from selecting the size of the print to choosing the type of framing or even tweaking the color palette. This level of personalization ensures that the art you bring into your home is not just a piece on the wall but a reflection of your unique taste and style.

Consider the joy of having a favorite quote overlaid on a serene landscape or a cherished family photo transformed into a gallery-worthy piece. Print on demand's commitment to customization allows you to infuse your personal touch into the art you choose, turning each piece into a conversation starter and a symbol of the stories that make your home uniquely yours.

The Future of Art: Print on Demand as a Catalyst for Change:

As we stand at the crossroads of affordability and elegance in art, print on demand emerges as a catalyst for change in the industry. This innovative approach has not only transformed how we acquire art but has also redefined the relationship between artists and their audience. It's a glimpse into the future where art is not confined to elite circles but is a shared experience, a collective celebration of creativity and expression.

The future of art with print on demand is a landscape where artists have the freedom to create authentically, where art enthusiasts can explore without financial barriers, and where the walls of our homes become vibrant canvases that tell stories, evoke emotions, and spark conversations. The democratization of art through print on demand is not just a trend; it's a shift in paradigm that heralds a more inclusive, diverse, and accessible era for the world of art.

Conclusion:

In the grand tapestry of art, print on demand has woven a thread of accessibility, affordability, and elegance. The walls of your home can now be adorned with pieces that tell stories, stir emotions, and reflect your unique taste, all without draining your wallet. As print on demand continues to reshape the landscape of the art world, we find ourselves at the forefront of a revolution where art is no longer a privilege but a shared joy for everyone to embrace.

NAUTICAL NODS: SAILING INTO COASTAL SERENITY WITH MARINE-THEMED ART

Ahoy, decorating enthusiasts! Get ready to embark on a sea-inspired journey as we delve into the world of "Nautical Nods." In this blog post, we'll explore how marine-themed art can effortlessly bring the calming vibes of the coast into your home. From ship wheels to oceanic hues, we'll uncover the secrets of creating a coastal paradise that will make you feel like you're living by the beach, no matter where you are.

SETTING SAIL WITH NAUTICAL COLORS

Our first stop, "Setting Sail with Nautical Colors," takes us on a voyage through the oceanic color palette. Dive into the soothing tones of navy blues, serene whites, and sandy beiges that evoke the essence of the sea. Whether you're choosing wall art, throw pillows, or decorative accents, opt for pieces that capture the tranquil hues of the coastal landscape.

Consider incorporating artwork featuring shades of azure and turquoise to set the stage for your nautical theme. The use of nautical colors creates an instant connection to the seaside, transforming your living space into a haven of coastal tranquility.

Navigating Style: Choosing the Right Nautical Art Pieces

In "Navigating Style," we explore the diverse range of nautical art pieces that can elevate your coastal decor. From classic ship paintings to contemporary maritime photography, the options are as vast as the open sea. Learn how to choose art that aligns with your personal style while staying true to the nautical theme.

Consider incorporating a statement piece, such as a vintage ship wheel or a collection of framed nautical maps, to anchor your decor in maritime elegance. Navigating style ensures that your choice of nautical art not only complements your space but also becomes a captivating focal point that tells a story of maritime adventure.

Seaside Elements: Incorporating Nautical Decor

In "Seaside Elements," we explore how incorporating nautical decor elements can transport your home to the coast. From anchor motifs to rope accents, discover how these subtle nods to the sea can enhance the overall nautical theme. Learn how to strike a balance between marine-inspired details and a cohesive design that reflects your taste.

Consider adding rope-wrapped vases, anchor-shaped bookends, or even a ship-shaped mirror to infuse your space with authentic seaside charm. The incorporation of seaside elements ensures that your home reflects the essence of coastal living, creating a harmonious and inviting atmosphere.

DIY Coastal Crafts: Personalizing Nautical Decor

"DIY Coastal Crafts" invites you to embark on a creative journey as we explore simple and personalized ways to add nautical flair to your decor. From crafting your own sailor's knots to repurposing driftwood into wall art, discover how easy and enjoyable it is to infuse your home with handmade coastal charm.

Consider creating a beach-inspired gallery wall using DIY seashell frames or personalized buoy art. Engaging in DIY coastal crafts not only adds a unique touch to your decor but also allows you to express your creativity while embracing the relaxed spirit of coastal living.

Bringing the Outdoors In: Nautical Gardens and Terraces

In "Bringing the Outdoors In," we step outside to explore how nautical decor can seamlessly extend into your gardens and terraces. From weathered anchor planters to maritime-themed outdoor rugs, learn how to create an outdoor oasis that mirrors the tranquility of coastal landscapes.

Consider adorning your outdoor space with marine-inspired patio furniture, adorned with nautical cushions and throws. Bringing the outdoors in ensures that your love for the sea extends beyond your living room, creating a cohesive and inviting atmosphere throughout your entire home.

Anchored in Serenity: Transforming Bedrooms with Nautical Themes

Our final destination, "Anchored in Serenity," focuses on transforming bedrooms into serene coastal retreats. Explore how to incorporate nautical elements into bedding, wall art, and decor to create a space that lulls you into restful slumber with the calming whispers of the sea.

Consider choosing crisp white bedding with navy blue stripes or opting for a statement headboard featuring a maritime print. Anchored in serenity ensures that your bedroom becomes a haven of coastal calm, inviting you to unwind and dream of the open ocean.

Conclusion:

As we conclude our nautical adventure, remember that the beauty of marine-themed art lies in its ability to transport you to the serene shores of the coast. Whether you're setting sail with nautical colors, navigating style with the right art pieces, incorporating seaside elements, engaging in DIY coastal crafts, bringing the outdoors in, or anchoring your serenity in bedrooms, each section unveils a facet of the transformative power that nautical decor holds in creating a coastal paradise within your home.

PIXELS AND PROGRESS: ELEVATING GAMING AND TECH SPACES WITH FUTURISTIC ART FOR INNOVATORS

The Canvas of the Future in Gaming and Tech Spaces

Embark on a journey into the future where pixels meet progress, and tech spaces become canvases for futuristic artistry. In this blog post, we'll explore the dynamic intersection of gaming and technology with forward-thinking businesses that leverage futuristic art to create immersive environments. From cutting-edge installations to digital masterpieces, discover how the art of the future is transforming gaming and tech spaces.

Pixels in Harmony - The Artful Integration of Technology

Pixels in Harmony sets the stage for our exploration, highlighting the artful integration of technology into gaming and tech spaces. Modern businesses recognize the importance of blending art seamlessly with technology to create immersive and visually stunning environments. Consider LED walls that respond to user interactions, creating a dynamic visual experience. Embrace digital canvases that showcase futuristic animations, transforming spaces into interactive realms where art and technology coalesce.

The artful integration of pixels not only enhances the aesthetic appeal but also contributes to the overall user experience. Imagine a gaming lounge where walls come alive with vibrant pixel art, reacting to the energy of the players. By harmonizing pixels and technology, businesses cultivate environments that captivate, inspire, and push the boundaries of what's possible in gaming and tech spaces.

VR Vistas - Navigating Virtual Worlds Through Art

VR Vistas unfolds as a chapter dedicated to navigating virtual worlds through art, transforming gaming and tech spaces into gateways to unexplored realms. Virtual Reality (VR) spaces are not just about cutting-edge technology; they are also opportunities for artistic expression. Consider VR installations that transport users to visually stunning landscapes or immersive digital galleries. These spaces become canvases for artists to craft experiences that transcend physical limitations, offering users a journey through the extraordinary.

Collaborate with digital artists to create VR environments that not only showcase their talents but also push the boundaries of what is conceivable in the virtual realm. VR Vistas redefine the concept of art spaces by allowing users to step into the artwork itself, blurring the lines between the physical and the digital. In this futuristic landscape, gaming and tech spaces become portals to endless possibilities where users can explore, interact, and be enveloped by art in unprecedented ways.

Augmented Realms - Enhancing Reality Through Art

Augmented Realms emerge as a captivating dimension where reality is enhanced through art, revolutionizing the way we perceive gaming and tech spaces. Augmented Reality (AR) technologies bring digital elements into the physical world, allowing businesses to overlay futuristic art onto real-world environments. Imagine a tech showroom where products come to life through AR animations or a gaming arena where players interact with augmented elements seamlessly integrated into the space.

The enhancement of reality through art not only provides an engaging experience for users but also serves as a tool for storytelling and brand expression. Businesses can leverage AR to create interactive exhibits, where users can unlock hidden art elements by exploring the space with their devices. Augmented Realms redefine the spatial experience, turning gaming and tech spaces into dynamic environments that transcend the traditional boundaries of art and reality.

Neon Horizons - Illuminating Spaces with Futuristic Illumination

Neon Horizons light up the narrative, showcasing the transformative power of futuristic illumination in gaming and tech spaces. Neon lights have long been associated with futurism, and businesses are embracing this aesthetic to elevate their spaces. Consider neon installations that outline the contours of gaming stations, futuristic sculptures that emit ethereal glows, or immersive LED ceilings that mimic the night sky. Neon Horizons bring an otherworldly ambiance to gaming and tech spaces, creating an atmosphere that feels straight out of a cyberpunk dream.

The use of neon and futuristic illumination not only adds a visual spectacle but also reinforces the theme of innovation and progress. These vibrant lights turn gaming lounges into dynamic landscapes, and tech offices into energized hubs of creativity. Neon Horizons transform spaces into futuristic realms where the interplay of light and art becomes an integral part of the user experience.

Interactive Installations - Bridging Play and Art

Interactive Installations bridge the gap between play and art, creating dynamic spaces that respond to user engagement. Businesses are incorporating installations that invite users to interact physically with the art, blurring the lines between observer and participant. Consider touch-sensitive walls that react to gestures, interactive floors that respond to movement, or even collaborative installations where multiple users can contribute to a digital masterpiece. These installations redefine the relationship between users and art, transforming gaming and tech spaces into dynamic playgrounds of creativity.

The integration of interactive elements not only enhances user engagement but also fosters a sense of ownership and connection. Users become active participants in the artistic experience, influencing and shaping the evolving artwork in real-time. Interactive Installations turn gaming and tech spaces into arenas of co-creation, where users are not just consumers of art but collaborators in the artistic process.

Futuristic Expression - Crafting Identity in Gaming and Tech Spaces

As the final stroke on the canvas of futuristic art in gaming and tech spaces, Futuristic Expression becomes the theme that defines the identity of these innovative environments. Businesses are actively crafting their identities through artistic expressions that align with their brand narratives. Consider custom installations that reflect the ethos of a tech company, or gaming spaces adorned with futuristic murals that resonate with the gaming community. Futuristic Expression goes beyond mere decoration; it becomes a powerful tool for businesses to communicate their values, aspirations, and commitment to pushing the boundaries of technology and creativity.

Futuristic Expression not only defines the aesthetic character of gaming and tech spaces but also serves as a beacon that attracts like-minded individuals. Businesses become pioneers in crafting unique and identifiable spaces that resonate with the futuristic visions of their users. As gaming and tech spaces evolve, Futuristic Expression ensures that these environments not only keep up with the times but actively shape the narrative of the future.

PERSONALIZED PERFECTION: UNVEILING THE MAGIC OF CUSTOM MURALS FOR YOUR UNIQUE SPACE

Welcome to a world where your walls tell a story as unique as you are. In this blog post, we embark on a journey through the realm of custom murals, exploring how tailor-made art transforms your living space into a canvas that reflects your personality, passions, and dreams. From capturing cherished memories to bringing your wildest fantasies to life, custom murals invite you to break free from the ordinary and embrace a living environment that is uniquely, undeniably, and beautifully yours.

The Art of You: Expressing Personality Through Custom Murals

Dive into the first section, "The Art of You," where we delve into the transformative power of expressing your personality through custom murals. Unlike mass-produced art, custom murals allow you to infuse your space with elements that resonate with your character and experiences. Whether you're a free spirit craving abstract patterns, a nature enthusiast yearning for scenic landscapes, or a pop culture aficionado desiring iconic imagery, the possibilities are as limitless as your imagination.

Imagine waking up to a sunrise over your favorite vacation spot or being surrounded by a mural that encapsulates the essence of your most cherished memories. Custom murals become a visual diary of your life, narrating the story of who you are and what brings you joy. Embrace the art of you with murals that serve as an authentic reflection of your personality.

Tailoring Spaces: Custom Murals for Every Room

Move on to the second section, "Tailoring Spaces," where we explore the versatility of custom murals in transforming every room in your home. From the bedroom to the living room, kitchen, home office, or even the bathroom, custom murals offer a personalized touch to each space. Consider a calming nature scene for the bedroom, a vibrant abstract mural for the living room, or a motivational quote in the home office – each mural creates a unique ambiance tailored to the purpose of the room.

Break away from the one-size-fits-all approach to decor and let each room reflect its own personality. Custom murals become a seamless extension of your interior design, turning your home into a harmonious and cohesive living environment. Explore how the art on your walls can shape the energy of each space, making every room a personalized sanctuary.

Memory Lane: Capturing Moments with Personalized Murals

In the third section, "Memory Lane," we delve into the sentimental journey of capturing cherished moments with personalized murals. Imagine immortalizing a family vacation, a graduation ceremony, or a milestone celebration as a stunning mural that adorns your walls. Custom murals become a tangible celebration of the moments that matter most, creating a visual narrative that takes you down memory lane every time you glance at them.

Consider transforming a wall into a gallery of family photos, blending seamlessly into your decor. Personalized murals allow you to freeze time and relive precious memories in a way that transcends traditional photo frames. Explore how the art of capturing moments can turn your home into a living photo album, filled with the warmth of shared experiences.

Fantasy Walls: Bringing Dreams to Life with Custom Murals

Enter the fourth section, "Fantasy Walls," where we unlock the door to a realm of limitless possibilities. Custom murals offer a unique opportunity to bring your wildest dreams and fantasies to life on your walls. Whether it's a cosmic journey through space, an underwater world teeming with marine life, or a whimsical fairytale landscape, your imagination sets the boundaries.

Explore the magic of turning your bedroom into a celestial sanctuary or your child's playroom into a vibrant jungle filled with friendly animals. Fantasy walls not only add a touch of enchantment to your space but also serve as daily reminders of the dreams that inspire you. Unleash your creativity and discover how custom murals can turn your living space into a canvas for your most imaginative visions.

Collaborative Creations: Engaging Artists for Custom Murals

In the fifth section, "Collaborative Creations," we explore the exciting process of engaging artists to bring your custom mural visions to life. Collaborating with talented artists allows you to translate your ideas into breathtaking artworks that resonate with your vision. Whether you choose a local muralist, commission an online artist, or work with a creative agency, the collaborative journey becomes an integral part of the mural's story.

Share your inspiration, discuss concepts, and witness the transformation of your ideas into a visual masterpiece. Engaging artists for custom murals not only ensures a personalized touch but also supports the vibrant community of creatives who bring these imaginative visions to life. Discover the joy of collaboration as your walls become a canvas for shared artistic expression.

Timeless Treasures: Investing in the Longevity of Custom Murals

In the final section, "Timeless Treasures," we explore the enduring value of investing in the longevity of custom murals. Unlike transient trends, personalized murals stand the test of time, evolving with you as your tastes and preferences change. Consider custom murals as timeless treasures that grow alongside your life journey, becoming an integral part of your evolving story.

Explore durable materials and quality craftsmanship to ensure that your custom murals retain their vibrancy and beauty for years to come. Investing in the longevity of custom murals allows you to create a living space that is not only uniquely yours but also a testament to the enduring value of personalized art. Discover the joy of surrounding yourself with walls that age gracefully alongside you.

Conclusion:

As we conclude our exploration into the world of custom murals, remember that your walls are a canvas waiting to be transformed into a personalized masterpiece. From expressing your personality and tailoring spaces to capturing memories, bringing dreams to life, collaborative creations, and timeless treasures, each section has unveiled a facet of the magic that custom murals bring to your living space. Embrace the opportunity to make your walls uniquely, undeniably, and beautifully yours.

WHISPERS OF SERENITY: ELEVATING YOUR SPACE WITH PASTELS AND NEUTRALS

Step into a world of tranquility as we explore the subtle elegance of pastels and neutrals in home decor. In this blog post, "Whispers of Serenity," we'll unravel the magic of softening your space with subtle art. From the gentle strokes of pastels to the soothing embrace of neutrals, discover how these understated tones create an atmosphere of calmness and sophistication. Join us on a journey where whispers of serenity transform your living space into a haven of peace and timeless beauty.

Pastel Palette Paradise: Infusing Soft Hues into Your Decor

Begin our exploration in "Pastel Palette Paradise," where we dive into the gentle world of pastels. Soft hues like blush pink, mint green, and baby blue bring a sense of serenity and whimsy to any space. Whether through wall art, cushions, or decor accents, pastels have the power to uplift the mood and create a light-hearted ambiance.

Consider incorporating pastel art featuring abstract compositions or nature-inspired scenes. The versatility of pastels allows them to seamlessly blend into various decor styles, from modern to shabby chic. Immerse yourself in the soothing palette of pastels and witness how these delicate tones infuse your home with a sense of freshness and joy.

Neutrals Unveiled: The Timeless Charm of Soft Elegance

Transition into the realm of "Neutrals Unveiled," where we explore the timeless charm of soft elegance. Neutrals, including whites, beiges, and grays, provide a classic backdrop that transcends trends and fads. Soft neutral tones create a calming and sophisticated atmosphere, allowing other elements in the room to shine.

Incorporate neutral art pieces that showcase the beauty of simplicity and understated elegance. Consider minimalist line drawings, serene landscapes, or abstract compositions in neutral tones. Neutrals act as a blank canvas, allowing you to experiment with textures and shapes without overwhelming the senses. Delve into the world of soft elegance and discover the enduring appeal of neutral tones in your decor.

The Art of Subtlety: Balancing Pastels and Neutrals

In the third section, "The Art of Subtlety," we explore the delicate balance of combining pastels and neutrals in your decor. The key lies in creating a harmonious blend that exudes sophistication and serenity. Consider pairing pastel walls with neutral furniture or vice versa, allowing each element to complement the other seamlessly.

Artwork that seamlessly integrates both pastels and neutrals becomes the focal point in achieving this balance. Look for pieces that feature soft pastel accents against neutral backgrounds or vice versa. The art of subtlety allows you to create a space that feels cohesive and refined, where pastels and neutrals work in tandem to evoke a sense of calm sophistication.

Textures in Tranquility: Elevating Subtle Art with Tactile Elements

Move on to "Textures in Tranquility," where we explore how the addition of tactile elements elevates subtle art to a new level of sophistication. Incorporating textures such as linen, canvas, or even subtle metallic accents enhances the visual interest of pastel and neutral art pieces. The interplay of soft colors and tactile surfaces creates a sensory experience that adds depth to your decor.

Consider selecting art pieces that feature a mix of textures, inviting touch and exploration. From abstract paintings with layered brushstrokes to photography prints on textured paper, the possibilities are endless. Textures in tranquility transform your space into a haven of subtle opulence, where every glance and touch becomes a moment of serene indulgence.

Mixing and Matching: Curating a Gallery of Subtle Statements

Enter the fifth section, "Mixing and Matching," where we explore the art of curating a gallery of subtle statements. Create a visual feast by combining pastel and neutral art pieces in a curated gallery wall. The juxtaposition of soft hues and neutral tones adds depth and visual interest to your space, turning your walls into an ever-evolving masterpiece.

Experiment with different frame styles and sizes to create a balanced and dynamic composition. Mixing and matching subtle art allows you to showcase your personality while maintaining a cohesive theme. Dive into the world of curated galleries and witness how the thoughtful arrangement of pastel and neutral art transforms your walls into a captivating narrative.

Subtle Art DIY: Adding a Personal Touch to Tranquil Spaces

In the final section, "Subtle Art DIY," we explore the joy of adding a personal touch to tranquil spaces through creative and understated DIY projects. Unleash your creativity by crafting your own pastel and neutral art pieces, whether through abstract paintings, framed fabric art, or minimalist line drawings.

Consider involving family members in DIY projects, turning the creation of subtle art into a bonding experience. The beauty of DIY lies not only in the finished product but also in the process of self-expression and collaboration. Embrace the joy of crafting personalized art that adorns your walls with tranquility and a touch of your unique story.

Conclusion:

As we conclude our journey through the whispers of serenity in pastels and neutrals, remember that the true magic lies in the subtlety of these tones. Whether you're drawn to the pastel palette paradise, the timeless charm of neutrals unveiled, the delicate art of subtlety, textures in tranquility, mixing and matching curated galleries, or the joy of subtle art DIY, each section unveils a facet of the transformative power that pastels and neutrals hold in softening your space.

KITCHEN CANVAS: ART IDEAS FOR THE HEART OF YOUR HOME

Welcome to the heart of your home, where culinary creativity meets artistic expression in "Kitchen Canvas: Art Ideas for the Heart of Your Home." This blog post is a flavorful journey into transforming your kitchen into a vibrant and visually appealing space with the right art choices.

CULINARY CANVASES: ART THAT SPEAKS TO FOODIES

In "Culinary Canvases," we explore the delicious world of food-inspired art. From colorful fruit and vegetable prints to detailed culinary illustrations, discover how incorporating art that celebrates the joy of cooking can add a dash of personality to your kitchen. Culinary Canvases invites you to let your taste buds inspire your art choices and turn your kitchen into a culinary masterpiece. Consider framing vintage recipe cards or displaying whimsical utensil-themed art to infuse your space with the warmth of the kitchen.

Gallery of Memories: Personal Touches in the Kitchen

In "Gallery of Memories," we delve into the idea of turning your kitchen into a gallery of cherished memories. Explore how displaying family photos, snapshots of memorable meals, or travel-inspired art can create a personalized and heartwarming atmosphere. Gallery of Memories encourages you to curate a visual timeline that celebrates the moments and people that make your kitchen the heart of your home.

Consider creating a photo wall or incorporating a gallery shelf to display a rotating collection of memories, keeping your kitchen decor fresh and meaningful.

Culinary Color Palettes: Infusing Vibrancy into Your Space

In "Culinary Color Palettes," we explore the art of infusing vibrant colors into your kitchen. From bold abstract pieces to artwork inspired by fresh produce, learn how color can impact the overall mood and energy of your culinary space. Culinary Color Palettes encourages you to play with contrasting hues, creating a lively and visually stimulating atmosphere.

Consider selecting art that complements your kitchen's color scheme, whether it's a pop of citrus shades for a lively vibe or calming blues and greens for a more relaxed ambiance.

Functional Art: Blending Practicality with Aesthetics

In "Functional Art," we discover how to marry form and function in the kitchen. Explore the world of practical yet aesthetically pleasing art, such as chalkboard menus, magnetic spice racks, or decorative hooks for kitchen tools. Functional Art encourages you to think beyond traditional wall hangings and embrace art that serves a purpose in your culinary space.

Consider installing a pegboard with hanging pots and pans for both visual appeal and easy access to your kitchen essentials.

Statement Backsplashes: Turning Tiles into Art

In "Statement Backsplashes," we take a closer look at turning your kitchen backsplash into a work of art. Explore the idea of using vibrant tiles, mosaic patterns, or even hand-painted designs to create a stunning focal point. Statement Backsplashes guide you on how to elevate your kitchen decor by treating your walls as a canvas.

Consider selecting backsplash art that complements your overall kitchen theme, adding an extra layer of creativity to the heart of your home.

DIY *Kitchen Art: Crafting Your Culinary Creations*

In "DIY Kitchen Art," we wrap up our journey by encouraging you to roll up your sleeves and create your own culinary-inspired masterpieces. From simple canvas paintings to repurposed kitchen tools, DIY Kitchen Art provides creative and budget-friendly ideas to add a personal touch to your culinary space.

Consider involving the whole family in DIY projects, creating a collaborative art display that reflects the collective creativity of your home.

Conclusion:

As you savor the rich aromas and create culinary delights in your kitchen, let "Kitchen Canvas: Art Ideas for the Heart of Your Home" inspire you to adorn the heart of your home with creativity and warmth. Elevate your cooking experience with carefully curated art, turning your kitchen into a canvas that reflects the essence of your family and culinary passion.

HEALTH AND WELLNESS: CALMING ENVIRONMENTS THROUGH THOUGHTFUL WALL ART

Step into a world where tranquility meets creativity in our blog post, "Health and Wellness: Calming Environments Through Thoughtful Wall Art." Here, we explore the profound impact of art on creating serene spaces that contribute to overall well-being. From mindfulness to aesthetics, join us on a journey to discover how the thoughtful placement of wall art can transform your living spaces into havens of relaxation.

SERENITY IN BRUSHSTROKES: EMBRACING NATURE-INSPIRED ART

In "Serenity in Brushstrokes," we explore the calming influence of nature-inspired art on well-being. Dive into the world of soothing landscapes, botanical prints, and oceanic scenes that bring the outdoors inside. Learn how integrating nature into your living space through art not only enhances aesthetics but also promotes a sense of calm and connection with the natural world.

Consider incorporating nature-themed art to evoke a sense of tranquility, creating a serene backdrop for relaxation and stress reduction.

Mindful Minimalism: Creating Calm with Simple Elegance

Uncover the beauty of "Mindful Minimalism" as we delve into the principles of simplicity and elegance in wall art. Explore how minimalistic pieces, characterized by clean lines and muted colors, contribute to a clutter-free environment. Learn how thoughtful curation and strategic placement of minimalist art can foster a sense of calm, allowing for mental clarity and relaxation.

Consider adopting a minimalist approach to your wall art, emphasizing quality over quantity to create an environment that promotes mindfulness.

Harmony of Hues: Color Psychology for Wellness

In "Harmony of Hues," discover the transformative power of color psychology in promoting wellness. Explore the calming effects of soft blues, greens, and neutral tones, and how they can influence mood and stress levels. Delve into the art of color selection, understanding how the right hues on your walls can create a harmonious and soothing atmosphere.

Consider incorporating calming color palettes into your wall art choices to foster a tranquil environment that supports mental and emotional well-being.

Personal Retreats: Creating Meditation Corners with Art

Explore the concept of "Personal Retreats" as we guide you through the process of designing meditation corners enhanced by art. Learn how strategic placement of mindfulness-inspired pieces can turn a small corner of your living space into a sanctuary for reflection and relaxation. Uncover the art of combining meditation practices with visual aesthetics to create a personalized retreat within your home.

Consider dedicating a corner of your living space to meditation and complementing it with art that resonates with your spiritual and relaxation goals.

Wellness Galleries: Curating Art for Mental Health

In "Wellness Galleries," discover how to curate art collections that prioritize mental health and well-being. Explore the role of personal connections with art, emphasizing pieces that evoke positive emotions and memories. Learn how the stories behind the art you choose can contribute to a sense of purpose, mindfulness, and emotional balance.

Consider curating a wellness-focused art collection that reflects your personal journey and promotes positive emotions, turning your living space into a gallery of well-being.

Innovative Art for Relaxation: Light, Sound, and Texture

In "Innovative Art for Relaxation," we explore the intersection of technology and art to create immersive and calming experiences. Dive into the world of light installations, soundscapes, and textured art that engage multiple senses simultaneously. Learn how innovative approaches to wall art can provide a holistic and therapeutic environment conducive to relaxation.

Consider incorporating innovative art installations that combine light, sound, and texture to create a multisensory experience that promotes relaxation.

In Conclusion:

In "Health and Wellness: Calming Environments Through Thoughtful Wall Art," we've uncovered the transformative potential of art in fostering tranquility and well-being. From nature-inspired scenes to mindfulness corners, the blog post serves as a guide to curating spaces that prioritize mental and emotional health. Elevate your living spaces into havens of calmness and relaxation through the thoughtful placement of wall art.

BOHEMIAN RHAPSODY: EMBRACING FREE-SPIRITED WALL ART FOR BOHO INTERIORS

Step into the enchanting world of Bohemian Rhapsody, where free-spirited creativity meets vibrant expression in the realm of wall art. In this blog post, we'll take you on a journey through six sections that celebrate the eclectic and laid-back charm of boho interiors. From whimsical prints to textured tapestries, discover how to infuse your space with the unique character and bohemian flair that defines this style.

Boho Canvas: Exploring the Canvas of Bohemian Art

In "Boho Canvas," we dive into the diverse landscape of artistic mediums that define boho wall art. From canvas paintings to woven tapestries and macramé hangings, explore the rich textures and materials that capture the essence of bohemian style. Learn how the use of natural fibers, such as jute and cotton, contributes to the organic and earthy feel that is quintessential to boho interiors.

Consider incorporating oversized canvas prints with abstract patterns or opting for handcrafted tapestries that tell a story of craftsmanship and individuality. Boho Canvas sets the stage for an exploration of artistic freedom that transcends traditional boundaries.

Prints and Patterns Fiesta: Celebrating Boho's Love for Eclectic Designs

In "Prints and Patterns Fiesta," we revel in the vibrant and eclectic designs that define boho wall art. Discover the joy of mixing and matching prints, from geometric patterns to floral motifs, to create a lively and visually dynamic display. Embrace the philosophy that more is more, as boho interiors thrive on an abundance of colors and patterns.

Consider layering different prints through a gallery wall or choosing wall art featuring mandalas, paisleys, and other culturally inspired designs. Prints and Patterns Fiesta celebrates the freedom to express your individuality through a kaleidoscope of colors and patterns that characterize boho living.

Natural Elements Symphony: Bringing the Outdoors In

In "Natural Elements Symphony," we explore the bohemian love for bringing nature indoors through wall art. Delve into the use of botanical prints, wooden sculptures, and seagrass wall hangings that seamlessly blend with the outdoors. Learn how the incorporation of natural elements adds a touch of serenity and connects your space with the beauty of the earth.

Consider adorning your walls with framed pressed flowers, rattan wall decor, or wooden mandala art to infuse your boho interiors with a sense of tranquility and harmony. Natural Elements Symphony encourages you to let nature be a guiding force in your bohemian decorating journey.

Vintage Treasures: The Charm of Boho Antiques and Thrifted Finds

In "Vintage Treasures," we celebrate the charm of boho interiors by incorporating antique and thrifted wall art finds. Discover how vintage mirrors, eclectic frames, and repurposed materials contribute to the eclectic and nostalgic vibe that defines boho style. Learn the art of thrifting and upcycling to curate a collection of wall art that tells a story of bygone eras.

Consider scouring flea markets, thrift stores, and antique shops for unique pieces that add character and history to your bohemian haven. Vintage Treasures invites you to embrace the allure of the old and reimagine how antique wall art can seamlessly integrate into your modern boho space.

Global Nomad Tapestry: Embracing Cultural Diversity

In "Global Nomad Tapestry," we embark on a journey that celebrates the bohemian spirit of cultural diversity. Explore how wall art inspired by various global traditions, such as Moroccan rugs, Indian textiles, or African batik, can infuse your space with a sense of wanderlust and worldly charm. Learn how to blend these diverse elements harmoniously to create a well-traveled and bohemian ambiance.

Consider mixing and matching textiles, tapestries, and wall hangings from different cultures to create a visual narrative that reflects the global nomad within you. Global Nomad Tapestry invites you to embrace the melting pot of influences that define boho style.

DIY Boho Magic: Infusing Your Personal Touch

In "DIY Boho Magic," we empower you to infuse your personal touch into your bohemian haven through the magic of do-it-yourself wall art. Discover easy and creative DIY projects that align with the boho aesthetic, such as yarn wall hangings, handmade dreamcatchers, or personalized canvas paintings. Learn how the process of creating your own wall art contributes to the authentic and free-spirited atmosphere of boho interiors.

Consider hosting crafting sessions with friends or family to collectively create unique pieces that hold sentimental value. DIY Boho Magic encourages you to let your imagination run wild and be an active participant in the artistic expression that defines your bohemian sanctuary.

In Conclusion:

As we conclude our exploration of Bohemian Rhapsody, remember that boho interiors are an ever-evolving canvas of self-expression. Whether you're exploring the canvas of bohemian art, celebrating prints and patterns, harmonizing with natural elements, embracing vintage treasures, traveling the global nomad tapestry, or infusing DIY boho magic, each section contributes to the symphony of individuality that defines boho style.

ABSTRACT SYMPHONY: EMBRACING THE ARTISTIC CHAOS ON YOUR WALLS

Step into a world where colors collide, shapes dance freely, and emotions find expression without boundaries. In this blog post, we invite you to embrace the vibrant realm of Abstract Expressionism and discover how the artistic chaos of abstract art can transform your walls into a dynamic and captivating canvas. From the bold strokes of iconic artists to the limitless possibilities of contemporary abstract expressionism, join us on a journey of creative liberation where your walls become a celebration of artistic freedom.

CHAOS IN COLOR: THE VIBRANT PALETTE OF ABSTRACT EXPRESSIONISM

Dive into the first section, "Chaos in Color," where we explore the vibrant palette that defines Abstract Expressionism. Abstract artists use color as a powerful tool to convey emotions, ideas, and energy without the constraints of realistic representation. Bold reds, electric blues, and sunlit yellows collide on the canvas, creating a visual symphony that speaks to the soul.

Whether it's the fiery intensity of Franz Kline's black and white compositions or the dreamlike hues in the works of Willem de Kooning, each stroke carries a unique energy. Embracing the chaos in color allows you to infuse your space with dynamic vitality, transforming your walls into a kaleidoscope of emotions and artistic expression.

Freedom in Form: Liberating Shapes and Lines

Move to the second section, "Freedom in Form," where we delve into the liberating world of shapes and lines in abstract art. Abstract Expressionism celebrates the freedom to explore forms without the constraints of representation. Geometric precision, gestural spontaneity, or a harmonious blend of both – abstract artists play with form in ways that challenge traditional notions of structure.

Discover the captivating works of artists like Jackson Pollock, whose iconic drip paintings redefine the boundaries of form and composition. Incorporating abstract art into your space allows you to break free from conventional design, encouraging a sense of liberation and creativity. Let the shapes and lines on your walls tell a story of boundless exploration and artistic freedom.

Texture and Depth: Adding Dimension to Chaos

Enter the third section, "Texture and Depth," where we explore how abstract expressionism adds a tactile and dimensional quality to your living space. Abstract artists experiment with texture, layering, and mixed media to create works that go beyond the visual, inviting a sensory experience. From the impasto technique of thickly layered paint to the incorporation of unconventional materials, abstract art engages the sense of touch.

Consider artists like Mark Rothko, who used color fields to evoke emotional responses, or the textured works of Jean Dubuffet that seem to leap off the canvas. Integrating abstract art with texture and depth transforms your walls into a multisensory experience, inviting both the eyes and fingertips to explore the artistic chaos that lies beneath the surface.

Emotional Impact: Abstract Expressionism and the Power of Feelings

In the fourth section, "Emotional Impact," we delve into how Abstract Expressionism harnesses the power of feelings to create a visceral connection with the viewer. Abstract art has the ability to communicate emotions on a profound level, transcending language and representation. The chaotic yet intentional brushstrokes convey a raw and authentic expression of the artist's inner world.

Explore the emotionally charged works of artists like Lee Krasner or Clyfford Still, whose canvases pulsate with intensity. Infusing your space with abstract expressionism allows you to curate an environment that resonates with your own emotions. Let the chaotic beauty of abstract art serve as a mirror for your feelings, creating a powerful and personal connection with your living space.

Curating Chaos: Blending Abstract Pieces in Your Collection

In the fifth section, "Curating Chaos," we discuss the art of blending abstract pieces seamlessly within your collection. While the term "chaos" may suggest disorder, curating a collection of abstract art requires thoughtful consideration of balance and cohesion. Explore how different artists, styles, and color palettes can harmonize to create a visually engaging and dynamic gallery on your walls.

Consider the works of Joan Mitchell alongside those of Wassily Kandinsky, finding common threads or intriguing contrasts. The key is to embrace the chaos with intention, allowing each piece to contribute to the overall narrative of your art collection. Curating chaos becomes an art form in itself, giving you the freedom to experiment and create a space that reflects your unique artistic sensibilities.

Living with Abstraction: Bringing the Chaos Home

In the final section, "Living with Abstraction," we explore the practical aspects of incorporating abstract expressionism into your daily life. Abstract art isn't confined to gallery spaces – it's meant to be lived with, allowing the chaos to become a seamless part of your home. From choosing the right scale and placement to considering the interplay of natural light, discover how to make abstract art an integral part of your living space.

Consider creating a focal point with a large abstract canvas or integrating smaller pieces into a gallery wall. Embracing the chaos in your daily surroundings fosters a sense of creativity and openness. Let your walls be a testament to the artistic journey you embark on every day, inviting the ever-changing energy of abstract expressionism into your home.

In Conclusion:

As we conclude our journey into the world of Abstract Expressionism, remember that the chaos on your walls is a celebration of artistic freedom, emotion, and exploration. From the vibrant palette to the freedom in form, texture and depth, emotional impact, curating chaos, and living with abstraction, each section has unveiled a facet of this dynamic and captivating art movement. Embrace the chaos on your walls, let the colors and forms speak to you, and revel in the liberating energy of abstract expressionism.

BEYOND REALITY: ABSTRACT PHOTOGRAPHY UNLEASHED IN CAPTIVATING WALL ART

Embark on a visual journey as we explore the mesmerizing world of abstract photography and its transformative power when translated into captivating wall art. In this blog post, "Beyond Reality," we'll delve into the realm of emotions, colors, and shapes that abstract photography encapsulates, revealing how it can be the key to unlocking a new dimension of expression in your living space. From the avant-garde allure to the emotional depth, discover how abstract photography transcends the boundaries of traditional art and captures the essence of emotions.

Avant-Garde Allure: Embracing the Unconventional in Abstract Photography

Dive into the avant-garde allure of abstract photography, where we explore the liberation from traditional constraints. Abstract photography invites artists and viewers alike to break free from the literal and embrace the unconventional. Through experimental techniques such as long exposure, multiple exposures, and intentional camera movement, photographers create images that are more about emotion and less about representation.

The avant-garde allure of abstract photography lies in its ability to spark curiosity and interpretation. Each viewer may see something different, unlocking a personal connection with the art. Consider incorporating abstract photographs that challenge the norm, inviting conversations and contemplation as they adorn your walls. Embrace the avant-garde and bring a touch of the unexpected into your living space.

Emotional Depth: Conveying Feelings Through Abstract Imagery

Transition into the realm of "Emotional Depth," where we explore how abstract photography becomes a powerful medium to convey feelings and evoke emotions. Unlike representational art, abstract photography doesn't rely on depicting recognizable subjects; instead, it relies on the interplay of colors, shapes, and textures to communicate on a visceral level.

Artists often use abstract photography to express complex emotions, whether it's the tumultuous waves of a stormy sea or the tranquility of a serene landscape. When translated into wall art, these emotional depths have the potential to transform your living space into a sanctuary of contemplation and reflection. Consider selecting abstract photographs that resonate with your own emotions, creating a harmonious atmosphere that speaks to the soul.

Color Symphony: The Vibrant Palette of Abstract Photography

In the third section, "Color Symphony," we explore the vibrant palette that abstract photography brings to the forefront. Abstract photographers often play with bold colors, creating a symphony of hues that stimulates the senses. The expressive power of color in abstract photography allows for the creation of visually stunning pieces that can become focal points in your home.

Consider the impact of a large canvas featuring a burst of colors, seamlessly blending or sharply contrasting. The beauty of the color symphony lies in its ability to evoke specific moods and atmospheres, transforming your living space into a dynamic and visually engaging environment. Immerse yourself in the kaleidoscope of abstract photography and let the vibrant palette breathe life into your walls.

Shapes and Forms: The Artistic Geometry of Abstract Photography

Move on to "Shapes and Forms," where we explore the artistic geometry that abstract photography introduces to wall art. By focusing on shapes, lines, and forms, abstract photographers create compositions that challenge the viewer's perception of reality. From the fluidity of curves to the precision of angles, the world of abstract shapes becomes a playground for artistic expression.

Consider incorporating abstract photographs that play with geometric patterns or showcase the beauty of organic forms. The deliberate arrangement of shapes adds a layer of sophistication and complexity to your decor. Dive into the world of artistic geometry and let abstract photography transform your walls into a canvas of dynamic shapes and intriguing forms.

Textures Unleashed: Adding Depth and Dimension to Abstract Wall Art

Enter the fifth section, "Textures Unleashed," where we explore how abstract photography adds depth and dimension to wall art through the capture of textures. Whether it's the roughness of weathered wood, the smoothness of flowing water, or the intricate details of a textured surface, abstract photographers excel in highlighting the tactile qualities of their subjects.

Textures in abstract photography invite a sensory experience that goes beyond the visual. When translated into wall art, these textured compositions have the power to transform your living space into a haven of tactile richness. Consider selecting abstract photographs that showcase a variety of textures, creating a multi-dimensional and immersive environment within your home.

Gallery of Emotions: Curating Your Abstract Photography Collection

In the final section, "Gallery of Emotions," we explore the art of curating your own abstract photography collection. Building a gallery wall with a carefully curated selection of abstract photographs allows you to tell a story, express your personality, and create a cohesive theme in your living space.

Consider a mix of sizes, frames, and subjects that complement each other while maintaining a sense of diversity. The gallery of emotions becomes a personal and evolving narrative that can be adapted to suit changing moods and seasons. Embrace the joy of curating your abstract photography collection and witness how it transforms your walls into a dynamic and emotionally charged gallery.

In Conclusion:

As we conclude our exploration of abstract photography in wall art, remember that the beauty lies in its subjective nature. Abstract photography transcends the boundaries of traditional art, inviting viewers to interpret and connect with the emotions it conveys. Whether you're drawn to the avant-garde allure, emotional depth, color symphony, shapes and forms, textures unleashed, or the idea of curating your gallery of emotions, each section unveils a facet of the captivating possibilities that abstract photography holds for transforming your living space.

CONTRASTING TEXTURES: MIXING FABRICS AND ART FOR DYNAMIC DECOR

Welcome to the world of "Contrasting Textures," where we explore the artful fusion of fabrics and artwork to create dynamic and visually engaging decor. In this blog post, we'll delve into the harmonious relationship between various textures, uncovering the secrets to achieving a stunning and inviting living space. Join us on a journey through six captivating sections, each revealing the magic of blending fabrics and art for an interior that truly captivates the senses.

Texture Tango: The Dance of Fabrics and Art

In "Texture Tango," we embark on a dance of textures, discovering how different fabrics and art forms can harmonize to create a captivating visual experience. Explore the interplay between smooth and rough, soft and coarse, as we delve into the art of balancing contrasting textures. Learn how to select fabrics that complement your artwork, enhancing both the tactile and visual elements of your decor.

Consider pairing a plush velvet sofa with a bold, abstract painting or a textured fabric wall hanging to infuse your space with a sense of luxury and depth. Texture Tango invites you to embrace the beauty of opposites colliding in a dance of visual and tactile delight.

Cozy Canvas: Fabric Art and Warmth

In "Cozy Canvas," we explore the cozy side of contrasting textures by integrating fabric art into your decor. Discover the warmth and comfort that fabric-based artwork brings to your space, creating a snug and inviting atmosphere. From tapestries and woven wall hangings to fabric-covered canvases, this section unveils the diverse world of fabric-based art.

Consider incorporating a large textile wall hanging in warm tones to transform a blank wall into a cozy canvas that evokes a sense of hygge and comfort. Cozy Canvas invites you to envelop your living space in softness, turning your walls into a comforting haven.

Pattern Play: Mixing Textile Patterns with Art

In "Pattern Play," we dive into the world of textile patterns and their harmonious coexistence with various art styles. Explore the art of combining geometric prints, floral motifs, and abstract patterns with complementary artwork to achieve a dynamic and visually stimulating decor. Learn how to balance bold patterns with subtle art and vice versa, creating a layered and sophisticated look.

Consider pairing a vibrant, patterned area rug with a collection of framed artwork in coordinating colors, creating a harmonious interplay of patterns and artistic expression. Pattern Play encourages you to unleash your creativity and experiment with the endless possibilities of pattern and art fusion.

Textile Tapestry: Wall Art Beyond the Canvas

In "Textile Tapestry," we shift our focus to the versatility of fabric as a medium for creating unique wall art beyond traditional canvases. Explore the world of textile tapestries, macramé wall hangings, and fabric sculptures that add a touch of bohemian charm and texture to your living space. Learn how these textile masterpieces can serve as both art and functional decor elements.

Consider incorporating a large macramé wall hanging as a statement piece that introduces texture, movement, and a touch of handmade artistry to your walls. Textile Tapestry invites you to think beyond conventional canvases and embrace the richness of textile-based wall art.

Sensory Symphony: Fabrics and Art for Multisensory Appeal

In "Sensory Symphony," we explore the concept of creating a multisensory experience by combining fabrics and art. Discover how the tactile qualities of textiles enhance the visual appeal of artwork, creating a rich and immersive environment. From soft throw blankets draped over sofas to textured canvases, this section encourages you to consider the sensory impact of your decor choices.

Consider layering different fabrics, such as a plush rug, velvet throw pillows, and a linen wall hanging, to create a symphony of textures that engage both the eyes and the sense of touch. Sensory Symphony invites you to elevate your decor by appealing to multiple senses, fostering a deeper connection to your living space.

DIY Textile Art: Unleashing Your Creative Expression

In "DIY Textile Art," we empower you to unleash your creativity by incorporating handmade textile elements into your decor. Explore simple and exciting DIY projects, from fabric-covered canvases to hand-stitched wall hangings, that allow you to personalize your space with a touch of your artistic flair. This section provides inspiration and step-by-step ideas for creating one-of-a-kind textile art pieces.

Consider organizing a crafting session with friends or family to create personalized fabric art that reflects your unique style and adds a handmade touch to your living space. DIY Textile Art invites you to embark on a creative journey and infuse your decor with a sense of personal connection.

In Conclusion:

As we conclude our exploration of "Contrasting Textures," celebrate the dynamic synergy of fabrics and art in crafting a living space that stimulates the senses and reflects your individual style. Whether you're drawn to the Texture Tango, Cozy Canvas, Pattern Play, Textile Tapestry, Sensory Symphony, or DIY Textile Art, each section unveils a facet of this captivating design trend.

MASTERING THE ART OF FRAME SELECTION:

A COMPREHENSIVE GUIDE TO CHOOSING THE PERFECT FRAME FOR YOUR MASTERPIECE

Art is a powerful form of expression, and when you invest time, effort, and passion into creating a masterpiece, it deserves to be showcased in the best possible way. One often overlooked element in presenting art is the frame. The right frame can enhance the visual appeal of your artwork, elevate its presence, and complement its aesthetic. In this comprehensive guide, we will delve into the art of frame selection, exploring the various factors to consider and providing valuable insights to help you choose the perfect frame for your art.

Understanding the Importance of Frames

1. Artwork Style and Genre: - Consider the style and genre of your artwork. Different styles may call for specific types of frames. For example, ornate and intricate frames might complement traditional or classical pieces, while sleek and modern frames may suit contemporary art.
2. Color Palette: - Pay attention to the color palette of your artwork. The frame should complement and enhance the colors rather than clash with them. Consider whether a neutral frame, a contrasting color, or a matching shade would work best to achieve the desired visual harmony.

3. Material Matters: - Frames come in various materials, each with its own aesthetic appeal. Wood, metal, and plastic are common options. The choice of material can significantly impact the overall feel of the artwork. For instance, a rustic wooden frame might add warmth to a landscape painting, while a sleek metal frame could enhance the modernity of abstract art.

4. Matting Options: - Matting, the border between the artwork and the frame, can influence the visual impact. Choose between single, double, or even triple matting, considering the dimensions of your artwork and the desired emphasis. Matting also helps protect the artwork by preventing it from coming into direct contact with the glass.

5. Size and Proportion: - The size of the frame should be proportionate to the size of the artwork. A large, bold frame might overpower a small, delicate piece, while an inadequate frame may diminish the impact of a larger work. Strike a balance to ensure that the frame enhances rather than distracts from the art.

6. Conservation and Preservation: - If your artwork has significant value, either sentimentally or monetarily, consider conservation framing. This involves using acid-free materials and UV-protective glass to prevent fading and deterioration over time.

7. Environment and Display Location: - Consider where the artwork will be displayed. Different environments might require different framing choices. For example, a bathroom with high humid-

ity levels may necessitate anti-mold treatment on the frame.

8. Budget Considerations: - Frames come in a wide range of prices. Determine your budget early in the frame selection process, and explore options that align with your financial considerations. Remember that a well-chosen frame can enhance the perceived value of the artwork.

9. Custom vs. Ready-Made Frames: - Decide whether to opt for a custom frame or a ready-made one. Custom frames allow for a tailored fit to your artwork's specifications, while ready-made frames offer convenience and cost-effectiveness. Weigh the pros and cons based on your unique needs.

10. Personal Preference: - Trust your instincts and personal taste. The frame you choose should resonate with you and complement the essence of your artwork. Consider the emotional and aesthetic connection between the frame and the art it encapsulates.

Case Studies: Matching Frames to Artwork

To illustrate the principles discussed above, let's explore a few case studies:
1. Traditional Landscape Painting: - For a classic landscape painting, consider a wooden frame with intricate detailing. Opt for a neutral color that complements the earthy tones of the artwork. A single mat with a slightly lighter shade can add depth and draw attention to the painting.

2. Abstract Contemporary Art: - Contemporary art often benefits from sleek and minimalistic frames. A metal frame with clean lines can enhance the modern aesthetic. Consider omitting matting for a more streamlined look that directs focus solely on the artwork

.

3. Portrait Photography: - Black and white portrait photography may thrive in a simple black or white frame. Consider a narrow frame with a subtle texture to add a touch of sophistication. Matting can be used to create space around the photograph, adding emphasis without distracting from the subject.

Conclusion

Choosing the right frame for your art is a nuanced process that requires careful consideration of various factors. By understanding the interplay between the artwork, frame, and display environment, you can elevate your masterpiece and create a visually captivating presentation. Whether you opt for a traditional wooden frame, a sleek metal design, or a custom creation, the perfect frame enhances the aesthetic impact of your art, ensuring that it is showcased in a manner that does justice to your creative vision. Embrace the art of frame selection, and let your masterpiece shine.

THE ART OF SELF-EXPRESSION: PERSONALIZE YOUR SPACE WITH ART PRINTS

Are you looking to add a touch of personality and creativity to your living space? Look no further than art prints from Art For The Home and Office.

With their wide range of vibrant abstract designs, contemporary patterns, and modern illustrations, you can easily personalize your space and express your unique style.

Art prints have become increasingly popular in recent years, and for good reason. They offer an affordable and versatile way to decorate your home or office. Whether you're looking to add a pop of color to a neutral room or create a focal point in a bold space, art prints can help you achieve the look you desire.

One of the great things about art prints is the variety of options available. At Art For The Home and Office, you'll find a curated collection of prints that cater specifically to women aged 25 and older in the US and Canada. This means that you can easily find artwork that resonates with your personal taste and preferences.

When choosing art prints for your space, it's important to consider the overall aesthetic you're trying to achieve. If you prefer a more minimalist look, opt for abstract prints with clean lines and muted colors. On the other hand, if you're drawn to bold and vibrant designs, choose prints with bold patterns and bright hues.

Another factor to consider is the size of the prints. Larger prints can make a statement and serve as a focal point in a room, while smaller prints can be grouped together to create a gallery wall. Experiment with different sizes and arrangements to find what works best for your space.

Once you've chosen your art prints, it's time to think about how to display them. There are several options to consider, depending on your personal preference and the layout of your space. You can frame the prints and hang them on the wall, lean them against a shelf or mantel, or even use them as a backdrop for a styled vignette.

Don't be afraid to mix and match different prints to create a cohesive and personalized look. You can choose prints with similar color palettes or themes, or opt for a more eclectic mix of styles. The key is to choose prints that speak to you and reflect your personality.

In conclusion, art prints from Art For The Home and Office are a fantastic way to personalize your space and express your unique style. With their wide range of options and curated collection, you're sure to find artwork that resonates with you. So go ahead, unleash your creativity and transform your space with art prints.

TRANSFORM YOUR SPACE WITH MODERN ART PRINTS

Are you looking to add a touch of modern sophistication to your home or office? Look no further than the vibrant and eye-catching abstract art prints from Art For The Home and Office.

With their bold and dynamic brushstrokes in a variety of vibrant colors, these prints are sure to transform any space and create a visually stunning focal point. One of our favorite pieces is showcased in the imagebelow. This contemporary art print features a mesmerizing display of bold brushstrokes, creating a sense of movement and energy. The vibrant colors add a pop of color to any room, instantly brightening up the space.

The print is elegantly displayed in a sleek and modern black frame, adding a touch of sophistication to the overall aesthetic. So how can you incorporate these modern art prints into your own space? Here are a few ideas and tips to get you started:

1. Create a Gallery Wall: Mix and match different art prints from Art For The Home and Office to create a stunning gallery wall. Choose prints with complementary colors and styles to create a cohesive look. Hang them in a grid pattern or arrange them in a more organic and eclectic manner.

2. Make a Statement: Choose a large-scale art print to make a bold statement in your space. Hang it above your sofa or bed to create a focal point in the room. The vibrant colors and dynamic brushstrokes of these prints are sure to catch the eye and spark conversation.

3. Mix and Match: Don't be afraid to mix different art styles and themes. Pair a contemporary abstract print with a more traditional landscape or still-life print for an unexpected and eclectic look. The key is to find a common thread, whether it's color, style, or subject matter, to tie the pieces together.

4. Consider Scale: When choosing art prints for your space, consider the scale of the room and the furniture. A small print may get lost in a large room, while a large print may overwhelm a small space. Take measurements and visualize how the print will fit into the overall layout of the room.

5. Personalize Your Space: Art is a reflection of your personal style and taste. Choose prints that resonate with you and bring you joy. Whether you prefer bold and vibrant colors or more muted and subtle tones, Art For The Home and Office offers a wide variety of prints to suit your individual preferences.

Remember, art is meant to be enjoyed, so have fun with it! Experiment with different arrangements and styles until you find the perfect combination that transforms your space into a visually stunning masterpiece. With the modern art prints from Art For The Home and Office, you can create a space that is uniquely yours.

THE PERFECT ART PRINTS FOR MEN & WOMEN IN THEIR 30S

Are you a man or woman in your 30s looking to add a touch of sophistication and style to your home or office? Look no further than Art For The Home and Office's collection of art prints from their brand, FromThePurpleHouse.

In your 30s, you've likely established your personal style and are looking for ways to express it in your living or workspace. Art prints are a fantastic way to add personality and flair to any room, and Art For The Home and Office has curated a collection specifically with women like you in mind.

If you're a fan of abstract art, you'll be delighted by the vibrant and bold designs available. Abstract art allows for interpretation and imagination, making it the perfect choice for those who appreciate creativity and individuality. Choose from a variety of colors and patterns that will make a statement in any room.

For those who prefer a more contemporary style, Art For The Home and Office offers elegant and minimalist art prints that exude sophistication. These pieces are perfect for creating a clean and modern aesthetic in your space. With their simple yet striking designs, they will add a touch of class to any room.

If you lean towards a more modern style, you'll find art prints that perfectly capture the essence of this aesthetic. From geometric patterns to sleek lines, these prints will bring a sense of sleekness and innovation to your home or office. They are the perfect choice for women who appreciate clean lines and a minimalist approach to design.

One of the best things about Art For The Home and Office is that they offer print-on-demand art prints. This means that you can choose the size and format that best suits your space and preferences. Whether you're looking for a small print to add to a gallery wall or a large statement piece to be the focal point of a room, they have you covered.

As an online-only store, Art For The Home and Office makes it easy for you to browse and shop from the comfort of your own home. You can take your time exploring their collection and finding the perfect art prints that speak to you. With their focus on promoting print-on-demand art prints, you can be confident that you're getting a high-quality product that is made specifically for you.

So why wait? Elevate your space with the perfect art prints for men and women in their 30s from Art For The Home and Office's brand, FromThePurpleHouse. Shop now and bring a touch of beauty and inspiration to your home or office. With their wide range of styles and options, you're sure to find the perfect art prints that reflect your unique style and personality.

ELEVATE YOUR HOME DECOR WITH ABSTRACT ART

Are you looking to elevate your home decor and add a touch of sophistication and style to your space? Look no further than abstract art! Abstract art is a versatile and timeless choice that can instantly transform any room.

At FromThePurpleHouse, we offer a wide selection of print-on-demand art prints that are perfect for creating a modern and contemporary look in your home. Abstract art is known for its unique and non-representational forms, allowing for endless interpretation and personal connection. It can evoke emotions, spark conversations, and serve as a focal point in any room. Whether you're a fan of bold and vibrant colors or prefer a more subtle and minimalist approach, our collection of abstract art prints has something for everyone.

One of the great things about abstract art is its ability to complement a variety of interior design styles. If you have a minimalist or Scandinavian-inspired space, a black and white abstract print can add a touch of elegance and simplicity. On the other hand, if you have a more eclectic or bohemian style, a colorful and expressive abstract piece can bring energy and vibrancy to your room.

When choosing abstract art for your home, consider the size and scale of the piece. A large, statement-making print can be the focal point of a room, while smaller prints can be grouped together to create a gallery wall. Don't be afraid to mix and match different sizes and styles to create a visually interesting and dynamic display.

In addition to size, consider the color palette of the artwork. If you want to create a calming and serene atmosphere, opt for prints with soft and muted colors. On the other hand, if you want to make a bold statement, choose prints with vibrant and contrasting colors.

Remember, abstract art is all about personal expression, so choose colors that resonate with you and your space. At FromThePurpleHouse, we understand that art is a personal choice, and that's why we offer a wide range of abstract art prints to suit every taste and style. Whether you're looking for a large canvas print for your living room or a smaller framed print for your bedroom, we have options that will enhance your space and reflect your unique personality.

So why wait? Elevate your home decor with abstract art from FromThePurpleHouse. Explore our collection today and transform your home into a work of art. With our print-on-demand service, you can easily order your favorite prints and have them delivered right to your doorstep. Start creating a space that is truly your own and let abstract art be the centerpiece of your home.

CREATE A SERENE ATMOSPHERE WITH NATURE-INSPIRED ART PRINTS

Are you looking to create a serene and peaceful atmosphere in your home or office? Look no further than Art For The Home and Office's collection of nature-inspired art prints.

Our online store, FromThePurpleHouse, offers a wide range of beautiful prints that bring the calming beauty of nature indoors. Nature has a way of soothing our souls and providing a sense of tranquility. By incorporating nature-inspired art prints into your space, you can create a serene atmosphere that promotes relaxation and peace.

Whether you prefer abstract, contemporary, or modern styles, we have the perfect prints to suit your taste. Imagine walking into a room adorned with a stunning print of a lush forest. The vibrant greens and earthy tones will instantly transport you to a peaceful oasis.

Or perhaps you prefer the calming effect of a tranquil lake scene, with its serene waters and gentle reflections. Our collection also includes breathtaking landscapes that capture the beauty of nature in all its glory.

One of the great things about art prints is their versatility. They can be easily hung on any wall, allowing you to transform your space in an instant. Whether you choose to display a single large print as a focal point or create a gallery wall with a collection of smaller prints, the possibilities are endless.

When selecting nature-inspired art prints, consider the mood you want to create in your space. If you're looking for a calming and soothing atmosphere, opt for prints with soft colors and gentle brushstrokes.

On the other hand, if you want to add a touch of vibrancy and energy, choose prints with bold colors and dynamic compositions.

Our nature-inspired art prints are specifically curated for women aged 25 and older in the US and Canada. We understand the importance of creating a space that reflects your personal style and promotes a sense of well-being. That's why we offer a variety of prints that cater to different tastes and preferences.

At Art For The Home and Office, we believe that art has the power to transform spaces and uplift spirits. By incorporating nature-inspired art prints into your home or office, you can create a serene atmosphere that promotes relaxation and rejuvenation.

So why wait? Visit our online store, FromThePurpleHouse, and explore our collection of beautiful prints today. Transform your walls and create a peaceful oasis in any room.

ART PRINTS THAT REFLECT YOUR UNIQUE STYLE AND PERSONALITY

Are you looking to add a touch of personality and style to your home or office? Look no further than our collection of vibrant and eye-catching art prints.

At Art For The Home and Office, we specialize in promoting print-on-demand art prints that are sure to reflect your unique style and personality. Take a look at the image below. Isn't it stunning?

This abstract art print is a perfect example of how art can transform a space and make a statement. The bold and vibrant colors immediately draw your attention, creating a visually striking composition. The mix of geometric shapes and fluid brushstrokes gives the artwork a contemporary and modern feel, making it a perfect fit for any modern space.

One of the great things about art prints is that they allow you to express your individuality and showcase your personal style. With our wide variety of themes and styles, you're sure to find something that resonates with you.

Whether you're into abstract art, contemporary designs, or modern aesthetics, we have something for everyone.

When choosing an art print, it's important to consider the colors and tones used in the piece. The colors in this particular print are a combination of warm and cool tones, adding depth and dimension to the overall composition. This creates a visually dynamic piece that will surely catch the eye of anyone who enters your space.

So, how can you incorporate art prints into your home or office?

Here are a few tips:

1. Choose the right size: Consider the size of your wall and the space you have available. A larger print can make a bold statement, while a smaller print can be a subtle addition to your decor.

2. Mix and match: Don't be afraid to mix and match different art prints to create a gallery wall. This can add visual interest and create a unique focal point in your space.

3. Frame it: Investing in a high-quality frame can elevate the look of your art print and make it stand out even more. Choose a frame that complements the colors and style of the print.

4. Consider the room's decor: Think about the overall style and color scheme of the room when choosing an art print. You want it to complement the existing decor and create a cohesive look.

DISCOVER THE BEAUTY OF CONTEMPORARY ART

Are you looking to add a touch of sophistication and creativity to your home or office space? Look no further than contemporary art prints! These vibrant and captivating pieces are the perfect way to showcase your unique style and add a pop of color to any room.
In this chapter, we will explore the beauty of contemporary art and provide you with some tips on how to incorporate it into your space.

Contemporary art is all about pushing boundaries and exploring new ideas. It is a reflection of the world we live in today, with its ever-changing trends and diverse cultures. The artwork showcased in the image below is a perfect example of contemporary art. Its bold and abstract shapes, combined with vibrant colors, create a visually stunning composition that is sure to catch the eye.

One of the great things about contemporary art is its versatility. Whether you prefer abstract, minimalist, or mixed media pieces, there is something for everyone. When choosing a contemporary art print for your space, consider the theme and style that best suits your taste. From abstract landscapes to geometric patterns, the options are endless.

When it comes to displaying your contemporary art print, the possibilities are endless. You can hang it on a blank wall to create a focal point in the room, or place it on a shelf or mantel for a more casual look.

Consider the size of the print and the space you have available when deciding on the placement. A larger print can make a bold statement, while a smaller print can be grouped with other pieces for a gallery wall effect. To enhance the beauty of your contemporary art print, consider framing it in a sleek and modern frame. This will not only protect the artwork but also add a touch of sophistication to your space. Choose a frame that complements the colors and style of the print, whether it be a simple black frame or a metallic finish.

If you're unsure of where to start when it comes to choosing a contemporary art print, consider browsing online stores like Art For The Home and Office. They specialize in promoting print-on-demand art prints and offer a variety of options with themes and styles that include abstract, contemporary, and modern. Our target audience is men and women aged 25 and older in the US and Canada, making it the perfect place to find a piece that speaks to your unique style.

In conclusion, contemporary art prints are a beautiful and creative way to add a touch of sophistication to your home or office space. Whether you prefer abstract, minimalist, or mixed media pieces, there is something for everyone.

Consider the theme and style that best suits your taste, and don't be afraid to experiment with different placement and framing options. With the right contemporary art print, you can transform any room into a visually stunning space that reflects your unique style and personality.

10 MUST-HAVE ABSTRACT ART PRINTS

10 MUST-HAVE ABSTRACT ART PRINTS TO ELEVATE YOUR HOME OR OFFICE SPACE

Are you looking to add a touch of modern and contemporary flair to your home or office space? Look no further! Art For The Home and Office presents "10 Must-Have Abstract Art Prints" that will transform any room into a vibrant and inspiring environment.

From vibrant colors to geometric shapes and expressive brushstrokes, these art prints are sure to captivate your imagination and elevate your space.

Let's dive into the top 10 abstract art prints that are a must-have for art enthusiasts and interior design lovers.

1. "Colorful Symphony": This art print bursts with vibrant colors, creating a symphony of hues that will instantly brighten up any room. Its abstract design adds a sense of energy and movement, making it a perfect centerpiece for your living room or office.

2. "Geometric Harmony": If you're a fan of clean lines and geometric shapes, this art print is for you. Its harmonious arrangement of shapes and colors creates a sense of balance and order, making it an ideal addition to a minimalist or modern space.

3. "Expressive Brushstrokes": For those who appreciate the beauty of expressive brushstrokes, this art print captures the essence of abstract expressionism. Its bold and dynamic strokes evoke emotions and create a captivating focal point in any room.

4. "Nature's Abstraction": Bring the beauty of nature indoors with this art print. Its abstract representation of natural elements, such as flowers or landscapes, adds a touch of serenity and tranquility to your space.

5. "Ethereal Dreams": Transport yourself to a dreamlike state with this ethereal art print. Its soft and delicate colors create a sense of calm and relaxation, making it a perfect addition to your bedroom or meditation space.

6. "Bold and Striking": Make a statement with this bold and striking art print. Its vibrant colors and strong lines demand attention, making it a perfect choice for a focal point in your living room or office.

7. "Abstract Cityscape": Capture the essence of urban life with this abstract cityscape art print. Its dynamic composition and use of colors reflect the energy and vibrancy of a bustling city, adding a modern touch to your space.

8. "Whimsical Delight": Add a touch of whimsy to your space with this delightful art print. Its playful shapes and cheerful colors will bring a smile to your face every time you look at it.

9. "Serenity in Chaos": Find beauty in chaos with this art print. Its intricate patterns and overlapping shapes create a sense of depth and complexity, making it a captivating addition to any room.

10. "Abstract Reflections": This art print invites you to contemplate and reflect. Its abstract composition and use of reflective surfaces create a sense of depth and introspection, making it a perfect choice for a medita-

tion or reflection space.

Conclusion:

Whether you're a seasoned art enthusiast or simply looking to enhance your home or office space, these 10 must-have abstract art prints from Art For The Home and Office are sure to inspire and captivate. From vibrant colors to expressive brushstrokes and geometric shapes, there's something for every taste and style. Visit our online store, FromThePurpleHouse, to explore our collection and find the perfect abstract art print to elevate your space.

AFTERWORD

At Art For The Home and Office, we understand the importance of finding art that speaks to you and reflects your unique style. That's why we offer a wide range of art prints that are sure to inspire and captivate. So go ahead, browse our collection and find the perfect art print to showcase your personality and style.

FromThePurpleHouse: Your Source for Stunning Art Prints

Are you looking to add a touch of elegance and sophistication to your home or office space? Look no further than FromThePurpleHouse, your go-to online store for stunning art prints. We specialize in promoting print-on-demand art prints with a wide range of themes and styles, including abstract, contemporary, and modern. Our curated collection is designed to cater to the tastes of men and women aged 25 and older in the US and Canada who appreciate the beauty of art.

Art has the power to transform any space and evoke emotions. It can be a reflection of your personality and style, and at FromThePurpleHouse, we understand the importance of finding the perfect piece to enhance your decor and express your unique taste. That's why we offer a carefully selected collection of high-quality art prints that are sure to impress.

Whether you're looking for a bold and vibrant abstract piece to make a statement, a contemporary print to add a modern touch, or a minimalist design to create a sense of calm, we have something for everyone. Our prints are created by Pictorem using the latest printing technology, ensuring that every detail is captured with precision and clarity. The colors are vibrant and true to life, making our prints a true work of art.

One of the advantages of print-on-demand art prints is that they are customizable. You can choose the size, frame, and even the type of paper to suit your preferences and the specific needs of your space. This allows you to create a truly personalized piece that fits perfectly into your home or office.

At FromThePurpleHouse, we believe that art should be accessible to everyone. That's why we offer competitive prices without compromising on quality. We work with a talented artist to bring you a diverse range of styles and themes, ensuring that there is something for every taste and budget.

Shopping for art prints online can sometimes be overwhelming, but our user-friendly website makes it easy to browse and find the perfect piece. You can search by theme, style, or even color, making it convenient to narrow down your options and find exactly what you're looking for.

Our detailed product descriptions and high-resolution images give you a clear idea of what to expect, so you can make an informed decision.

So why wait? Bring art into your life and transform your space with FromThePurpleHouse. Shop our collection of stunning art prints today and discover the perfect piece to enhance your decor and express your unique style. With our high-quality prints and affordable prices, you can create a beautiful and inspiring space that you'll love coming home to.

ABOUT THE AUTHOR

Neil J Milliner

Neil J. Milliner is a contemporary author, creative educator, and publisher focusing on helping creatives, introverts, and musicians build authentic brands, overcome perfectionism, and navigate career challenges through practical, psychology-backed guides. He writes books on music marketing (*The Musician's Marketing Playbook), songwriting (*Emotional Hooks Handbook), sustainable living, self-improvement (*How to Feel Better Without Fixing Everything), and building creative spaces. He runs his own imprint, Books by Neil J, and emphasizes connecting with one's core self for aligned, meaningful creation.

Key Themes in His Work:
- Authenticity: Building brands and creating music that reflects your true self.
- Overcoming Perfectionism: Practical strategies to move past creative blocks and endless tweaking.
- Music Industry Guidance: Marketing, songwriting, and technical advice for musicians.
- Mindful Living: Eco-habits and personal growth for creatives.

Who He Helps:
- Musicians, songwriters, producers
- Creative introverts
- Entrepreneurs and creatives seeking genuine connection
- Individuals wanting to live more sustainably